ATLAS of the
WORLD ECONOMY

ATLAS of the WORLD ECONOMY

Michael Freeman

Consulting Editor
Derek Aldcroft

SIMON & SCHUSTER
A Paramount Communications Company

New York   London   Toronto   Sydney   Tokyo   Singapore

First published 1991 by Routledge
11 New Fetter Lane, London EC4P 4EE

and in the USA by
Academic Reference Division
Simon & Schuster
15 Columbus Circle
New York, NY 10023
A Paramount Communications Company

Library of Congress Cataloging-in-Publication Data

Freeman, Michael J., 1950-
    Atlas of the world economy/Michael Freeman:
consulting editor, Derek Aldcroft.
      p. cm.
    Includes bibliographical references.
    ISBN 0-13-050741-5
    1. Economic history—1945–
    2. Economic indicators.
    I. Aldcroft. Derek Howard
    II. Title.
  HC59.F734 1991   90–26501
  330.9′04—dc20   CIP

ISBN 0–13–050741–5

Printed in England by Clays Ltd, St Ives plc

Contents

List of illustrations

List of plates

1 Burmese refugees in northern Thailand (Courtesy Nick Middleton)
2 Prairie farming in Oxfordshire, United Kingdom (Courtesy Tony Lee)
3 Cooling towers at Didcot coal-fired power station, Oxfordshire, United Kingdom (Courtesy Tony Lee)
4 Part of London dockland, once a mecca of manufacturing, but now largely de-industrialized (Courtesy Tony Lee)
5 Empty container ship at the port of Southampton, powerful symbol of the United Kingdom's massive trade deficit (Courtesy Tony Lee)
6 Liberian-registered tankers at the port of Southampton (Courtesy Tony Lee)
7 Migrant labourers at work on the ship-breaking beach at Gadani, Pakistan (Courtesy Nick Middleton)
8 Lower Manhattan, New York, USA (Courtesy Tony Stone Worldwide Photolibrary)

Foreword

Consciously or otherwise Michael Freeman's visual exposition of the world economy presents the reader with at least one striking theme, namely the dichotomy between the rich and poor nations of the world. A small group of highly developed countries with little more than 20 per cent of the world's population account for two-thirds or more of the world's energy consumption, manufacturing output, and merchandise trade. They also enjoy a comparable share of global income whereas over half the population of the world have to make do with incomes of less than $500 per capita (1984). The range is enormous, from a low of only $100 in the case of Ethiopia to $21,920 for the United Arab Emirates.

What is even more disconcerting, in view of the trend towards greater income equality in western countries in the present century, is that the distribution of income among nations may even have deteriorated during the past century. China and South east Asia, for example, probably had a more favourable world income share relative to their population than is the case today, while even by 1913 the rich nations of the western hemisphere (in North America and north-west Europe) accounted for at most some 60 per cent of global income.[1] One should of course heed the author's warning about the fragility of some of the statistical data, especially for earlier periods; even so it is doubtful whether more refined data would alter this broad conclusion significantly.

When one turns to the poorer nations in Latin America, Asia and, above all, Africa, there is almost a feeling of despair. How can they possibly escape from abject poverty when their populations are outpacing their resource base and when they are piling up debts that cannot be requited? Can they ever really hope to emerge from their 'gigantic backlog of backwardness'[2] into the world of modern economic growth? The task may appear to be insuperable, yet history demonstrates that countries in similar positions, that is in eastern Europe and the Pacific basin, have managed to do just that. History also suggests that lavish aid and credit from the west may not always be the crucial factor to achieve a breakthrough, since many Latin American and African countries borrowed heavily in the 1920s but with little visible effect on their development largely because the funds were squandered or misutilized.[3] Much in fact depends upon the type of government prevailing and it is at this point that Michael Freeman muses whether any of the known systems of political economy are relevant to some of today's African states. Systems which perpetuate gross income inequalities and favour corruption and graft are unlikely to provide the requisite conditions for dynamic change. The contrast between some of the corrupt Latin American states and the progressive countries in the Pacific basin region during the recent past is particularly instructive in this context.

A second major theme which emerges from this work is one concerning the use of resources. Western man has been profligate in the exploitation and consumption of the earth's resource base, so much so that this has evoked periodic alarms about the depletion and exhaustion of key resources at some time in the future. Energy has been the most frequently cited example both currently and in the past. The threat of an impending energy crisis may now have receded, but one resource often neglected, that of water, is already a major problem in some of the drier countries of the world and it could eventually pose a threat to some of the water-intensive economies of the capitalist west.

Yet resource deficiencies or resource depletion may in due course be superseded by an even more pressing problem, namely that concerning the environmental impact of man's continuing quest for economic advance. The intensive use of energy in the west and the rapid spread of its use elsewhere could in time raise environmental hazards which far transcend considerations of resource depletion and exhaustion. It is no doubt for this reason that Michael Freeman gives a veiled hint to the effect that environmental issues may well feature more prominently in later editions of his work.

This *Atlas of the World Economy* not only provides an excellent introduction to the global dimensions of economic activity, resource use, and the like, but at the same time it also gives the reader much food for thought as to the consequences of man's development over the last two centuries and the issues that are likely to loom large in the future. It is a very welcome addition to the literature on development and deserves to be widely consulted.

Derek H. Aldcroft
University of Leicester, November 1989

1 L.J. Zimmerman, 'The distribution of world income, 1860–1960', in E. de Vries (ed.), *Essays on Unbalanced Growth* (The Hague, 1962), pp. 54–5.

2 N. Spulber, *The State and Economic Development in Eastern Europe* (New York, 1966), p. 75.

3 See S.A. Schuker, *American 'Reparations' to Germany, 1919–1933: Implications for the Third-World Debt Crisis* (Princeton, 1988).

Preface and acknowledgements

This book was completed and ready for press before the dramatic events in eastern Europe of the late autumn and winter of 1989. The overthrow or capitulation of communist dictatorships in Romania, Czechoslovakia, East Germany and Bulgaria condensed into weeks changes which most western commentators had foreseen as requiring years to complete. Since the book is largely historical in its perspective, these events do not alter very much the picture that it provides, and not least because the data which are available on the former eastern block have typically been thin and in a form which often bears little comparison with the west. What is very clear, however, is that the extended trade relations between west and east, anticipated in the introductory discussion, are bound to accelerate. The desperate need for western investment aid to resolve chronic and often basic consumer shortages makes this inevitable. But beyond this, there remains an enormous arena for new systems and patterns of trading. The European Community seems likely to be at the forefront of such development, although the apparently inexorable pressures for German unification may re-cast the whole centre of gravity of the European trading realm.

The book was the idea of David Croom, now Managing Director of Routledge. To borrow his turn of phrase, it was intended to 'show how the world economy works'. I am not at all sure that the end-product has achieved what he had in mind, but it is the readers who will have the last verdict. The precise form of the book owes much to the demands of teaching one of the compulsory papers in the Geography Honour School at Oxford. My pupils at Worcester College and Mansfield College have been regularly plied with extracts as the book progressed. And they must be thanked for their tolerance and characteristic good humour, as well as their criticism. Derek Aldcroft has been an efficient and assiduous consulting editor, quick to counter my wilder assertions. Kenneth Warren, my colleague at Jesus College, read the entire manuscript and made many helpful suggestions. The graphics were drawn by Jayne Lewin with her customary patience and skill. Finally, I should record my thanks to Richard Stoneman, my editor at Routledge, for piloting the project through.

Michael Freeman
Oxford, February 1990

Introduction

To try to write about the world economy is to invite immediate criticism. In some eyes, *world economy* is merely a synonym for the western capitalist system which, over the course of more than half a millennium, has penetrated more and more corners of the globe in its search for continuing means of accumulation. Others will argue that the term fails to register the significance of the socialist states as a distinctive and largely separatist realm. Much the same might be said about parts of the African continent, where the living world is often far remote from the materialist culture of the west: western commentators may label such areas 'developing economies', but in many ways this is to invoke a datum which bears limited relevance to human existence there.

These inadequacies emerge yet more sharply when one begins to try to assemble data with which to chart the evolution of the world economy, especially since the Second World War. The most comprehensive and accurate data sets relate largely to the capitalist west. To the cynical observer, this is mainly because the capitalist realm is so preoccupied with its own economic performance. Capitalism appears to have no *steady state*. Change is its prevailing feature and thus the desire to monitor the path of change has become very strong. Less critical commentators see data collection as an integral part of economic and social planning and as a means of learning. But whatever the view, there can be no doubting the contemporary prominence and influence of international data-gathering bodies such as OECD, the World Bank, or the UN. It

is these organizations which largely determine the way we view the world economy. The World Bank, for instance, has as one of its primary categorizations the level of income per capita. The states of the world are then grouped into low-, middle- and high-income classes, implying a gradation in levels of income per capita. However, the data actually show a very high degree of skewness towards the lower end of the scale. Indeed, it is hard to avoid the conclusion that low-income states and many of the middle-income states are in fact a species of their own. Thus one might be drawn to question an approach which casts them in a perspective set largely by high-income states. If developing nations had their own equivalent of the World Bank, one is bound to ask how far its approaches and perspectives would differ. Equivalent problems are also apparent in relation to the World Bank's treatment of the socialist realm.[1]

None of this is necessarily to reject the formidable data records which world organizations like the World Bank gather. It is simply to underline the relational frame in which most of those data are set. For, ultimately, this is the material with which anyone examining the world economy has to work. If we cannot evade the biases of the capitalist world view, we can at least try to be doubly aware of its intrinsic character.

It is commonly said that you can prove anything with statistics. At the time that this introduction is being written (Spring 1989), the United Kingdom government is reviewing the way in which the monthly trade figures are calculated; some commentators expect that as a result the current-account deficit for 1988 will be reduced by between two and four billion pounds. A favourite trick among politicians when seeking to represent their government's record of improvement in the best possible light is to calculate from the base year which yields the highest order of change against the present. Where time-series statistics show considerable annual fluctuation, this can give rise to the most misleading of assertions. As far as the contents of this book are concerned, two major questions arise over the use of statistics. The first concerns their accuracy, including the way in which figures on particular issues are calculated. The second concerns the facility which exists for comparisons over space and over time.

Problems of accuracy are undoubtedly at their most acute when dealing with material for the developing world. The UN assembles annually one of the most comprehensive sets of demographic statistics for developing countries, but they are reliant for the most part on data submitted by governments and other agencies in those developing areas. Some investigators have found serious flaws and errors in certain of these data and in the methods of their compilation.[2] At an aggregate level, however, there is very little that can be done to check upon the representativeness or veracity of data. If one is seeking to use such UN data series, all that can be done is to allow for margins of error and to treat aberrant values very carefully. Sometimes it is the case that aberrant data sets reveal themselves, when, for example, one begins to try to interpret material or when comparison is made with similar sets elsewhere. In the developed world, although statistical series are universally more reliable, it is nevertheless true that problems still occur. In industrial production one can find instances where two reputable organizations publish substantially different totals for a single commodity sector for one and the same year.[3] Sometimes it is clear that the two are not measuring quite the

same thing; at other times, the discrepancy is inexplicable. It is generally true that the scale of variation in such cases is small, but it nevertheless underlines the fallibility of *all* statistics.

In the socialist world, notably in the USSR and eastern Europe, the statistical record has a peculiar twist of its own in that some of the freely accessible data series relate to plan targets. This applies especially in production statistics and, as a rule, such data are recognizable by their rounding. In theory, there is every reason to take such evidence at its face value; in practice, we know that plan targets are sometimes not achieved. For this reason, it has not been possible for the socialist world to feature in some sections of this book.[4] And in a wider sense, of course, there are many standard measures of capitalist world development for which no replicates exist in socialist realms.[5] This has given rise to yet further omissions.

Aside from matters of accuracy and reliability, the value of statistical data hinges very much on the form in which they are cast. When this atlas was first conceived the intention was to present a picture of the world economy as it evolved over the three decades from 1950 to 1980. In a limited number of cases this has been achieved, but in many it has not. The basic reason is that those who gather statistics do not necessarily have such an objective high in their sights. Rarely are the characteristics of data sets continuous over such a long time-span: data-collection methods alter and are improved; presentational bases are changed. Moreover, where it is actually the intention to monitor historical trends, the convention is to use index values, calculated in relation to a single-year base and not normally for much longer than a ten-year period. Naturally, it is impossible to compare, directly, two separate sets of index values for two separate time-periods. Given sufficient resources, there is little reason to doubt that one could, in fact, generate a fully comprehensive statistical base for most dimensions of the world economy as they evolved over the period from 1950 to 1980. However, this was far from the scope of the present project, which has sought its statistical information largely from existing statistical compendia.

Comparisons across space are as problematical as comparisons over time. The countries of the world do not, for instance, all take population censuses at the same time. In the developing world, the variability is especially acute; there are also some states where the latest available census material is more than a decade old.[6] When making comparisons between continents, such weaknesses are restricted in their force. But within continental masses, especially in the developing world, great caution is needed. In the specific case of demographic data, the general practice in this book has been to omit data entries which are not compatible by decade. Thus, for example, African states whose latest population statistics relate to censuses taken in the 1970s do not feature in population analyses which focus on the early- to mid-1980s. Organizations such as the UN attempt to deal with these incompatibilities by estimation, but not normally across the complete data range. Beyond relatively simple matters like differing dates of censuses, there are a host of problems over the different ways in which data are recorded in different states across the world. The position is perhaps most complicated in agricultural land-use, and once again it is in the developing world that most questions arise. Cropping patterns and practices often do not admit of the hard-and-fast classifications in conventional use in the developed west. Pastoral land-use presents almost intractable problems because of widely differing intensities and frequencies of grazing.[7] But even in the planting of high-yielding varieties of food grains, it is remarkable to discover that international statistics are scarce. Neither the FAO's production yearbooks nor its periodic

reports, *The State of Food and Agriculture*, carry data on HYVs. This is presumably because compatible sets of statistics simply do not exist, although it has not prevented authors from attempting to assemble series from different national sources.[8] What all this means, essentially, is that most sections of the book fail in some way to cover the full range of central issues. Textual reference is made to the majority of them, but clearly not to the same extent as would apply with suitable statistical series.

No book should concentrate in its beginning exclusively on apologia. What, then, does it go on to tell us about the broad face of the world economy in the post-war era? The outstanding feature of virtually every major theme addressed in the book is growth, be it of population, food supply, industrial goods, energy production, or whatever. The scale of growth naturally varies enormously, but few of the world's states have failed to share in it. Equally, however, a slowing down of growth has been an overriding characteristic of the world in the most recent two decades. This has been true in population, in energy consumption, and in a whole range of measures of economic output. Certain facets of this deceleration are viewed with almost unanimous support. The slowing down of the rate of world population growth is the primary example, but more efficient resource utilization among developed nations has helped to mollify fears about imminent crises in the ability of the planet to support mankind. The same cannot be said, however, for the slowing down of capitalist growth in the 1970s and 1980s. This has presented many western states with mounting problems of unemployment and has led to the growth of budget deficits as the costs of social welfare have run ahead of growth in taxation income. For private companies, meanwhile, declining rates of profit have precipitated not only plant closures and the lay-off of workers, but searches for ways of maintaining profit margins through new products, new technologies, new markets and new modes of production organization. The rise of industrial and conglomerate multinational firms is viewed by many as providing one of the clearest measures of the stresses upon the capitalist realm since the early 1970s. The force of the nation-state as an economic unit has been increasingly eroded as capital has sought out new arenas of investment which transgress the familiar political divisions of the free world. It is in this sense, perhaps above all others, that one can begin to talk of a *world economy*. It was the emergence of international oil companies which first signalled this trend in economic organization. But the oil industry's transnational format derived as much from the mismatch between the geography of production and that of consumption, whereas more recent transnational economic organization has its roots more firmly in the evolving imperatives of capitalist development. In part, it is also a creation of the formidable advances in information technology which allow prices and markets to be monitored simultaneously across the world, a facility which has, in tandem, helped to create a transnational sector in banking, insurance, and other business services.

If, as the pundits say, capitalism caught cold in the wake of the 1970s oil crises, one can hardly say that this applied to all of the world's major capitalist states. In this respect the record of Japan is legion. Devastated by defeat in war, with its scheme for a land empire in Southeast Asia in total ruin, Japan has, against all odds, managed to create an economic empire with an apparently unstoppable momentum. Its manufactured goods have penetrated most parts of the developed world to the extent that some governments have felt forced to apply import quotas upon them. From the 1970s, it also became a major foreign direct investor, in some instances largely as a means of side-stepping such import restrictions. However, banking now lies at the forefront of Japan's overseas interests and has become associated in particular with the acquisition of land and property. Los Angeles provides one of the most publicized examples of this development, with extensive tracts of its downtown area in Japanese ownership.[9] Almost as good a match for Japan has been the record of West Germany. Although not in any way insulated from the effects of depression, the vigour of its manufacturing base, particularly that for export, has carried it through where other states have faltered.

Aside from the phenomenon of growth, no reader of this book will escape the formidable dominance of the United States of America as a world economic force. Its share of world manufacturing output, for example, is roughly equivalent to that of all the countries of the developing world put together, its consumption of oil roughly twice that of the USSR. It is the world's largest single net exporter of grain, amounting to around 5 per cent of annual world consumption. Its GNP per capita is exceeded only by Switzerland and is half as much again as Japan's. It accounts for almost half of all outgoing foreign direct investment in the world and, in turn, is the recipient of roughly a third of the entire world's incoming FDI. It is against such a background that US economic commentators can fight shy of a budget deficit of 200 billion dollars at the opening of the Bush presidency. Relative to the overall strength and capacity of the US economy, the figure is miniscule; and the willingness of Japanese investors to underwrite the debt underlines the case. It may well be that American economic growth has been shaken over the past two decades, but the sheer magnitude of the American economy, as producer and as consumer, has been barely diminished. And given its assets of cultivated land, minerals, and other resources, let alone its control over similar assets overseas, the prospect is one of little change.

For many of the peoples of the Third World, the attainments of the American economy and its pivotal position in the workings of capitalism are remote. But it remains true that most states of the Third World have become locked into the capitalist system, both as a legacy of the production and trade dispositions established under colonialism and as a result of large-scale borrowings from western financial institutions against the security of agricultural exporting capacities or indigenous resources like oil and copper. These facets are apparent in various parts of this book. Whether they can be construed as favourable is a hotly contested issue. In Africa, for example, falls in leading world commodity prices, beginning in the 1970s, have seriously undermined the ability of many governments to service their foreign borrowings. By the mid-1980s, the low-income states of Africa had an average ratio of debt to GNP in excess of 50 per cent. The survival of trade and production from the colonial era has prompted critics to coin the label 'neo-colonialism', especially given the way in which the control of some export sectors has fallen into the hands of a select few multinational firms. Hence the familiar gibe is that one mode of exploitation has been replaced by another. Public aid programmes from the west, administered through such bodies as the World Bank, have themselves sometimes had deleterious repercussions. Aid for extensions of cash-crop production has, in some cases, depressed prices: the increased volume has not been matched by a corresponding increase in demand. Some industrial projects have involved too great a dependence upon imported materials, contributing to already unfavourable balance-of-payments deficits.[10] In the specific case of Africa, moreover, these various developments have come to figure against the insecure backdrop of serious drought and civil unrest.

In those states of the developing world where economic performance has been more successful, the particular weakness of capitalist organization has been its tendency to reinforce already unbalanced national income distributions. Several of the leading states of South America, Peru and Brazil among them, illustrate this point forcibly. In situations of poverty and underemployment, the labouring class has little power of protest. Wages and conditions remain exceptionally poor relative to the earning power of the production system, especially in sectors where goods are destined for western markets and hence western price levels.

If capitalist organization and interrelations can be seen as antagonistic to Third World development, it has to be said that forms of socialist organization have fared little better. In Marxist Ethiopia, agricultural performance has deteriorated since the institution of state collectivization and price-control policies, albeit against a background of environmental instability and civil war.[11] In Tanzania, state policies have generally perpetuated rather than eradicated pre-existing inequalities of rural income: the state as champion of the peasant interest appears to be a myth.[12] One is tempted to ask, therefore, whether *any* of the principal systems of political economy in practice in different parts of the world are relevant to areas like Africa. Indeed, the increasing consensus among many economists, politicians, and development strategists is that solutions to the dilemmas of many of the poorest developing states can be found only *within* the existing practices and institutions of those states.[13] Attempts to graft novel systems on to them, however workable elsewhere, have almost always met with undesirable, often unforeseen, consequences. And given the increasing divergence of many of the world's poorest nations from a normative pattern of evolution, this is perhaps hardly surprising. In many sections of this book, whether dealing with population growth, food production, debt, energy consumption, or whatever, these nations emerge as an increasingly isolated group, a world after their own image.

This introductory comment would be

incomplete without some reference to the so-called Second World: the USSR and the socialist states of eastern Europe and East Asia. As already discussed, our knowledge of the economies of many of these states is sometimes superficial in the extreme and also too readily examined through capitalist lenses. From the limited data available, though, some broad conception of the resource wealth of major world powers like the USSR and China is attainable. The USSR, in particular, stands out as a formidable reservoir of basic energy resources and of raw materials for industry. China boasted the world's largest coal industry by the 1980s and the most heavily trafficked of the world's railway systems in the internal movement of freight. China's family-limitation policies have also (reputedly) grappled successfully with its burgeoning population;[14] although as this is being written, it appears that the country will overshoot its planned population target for the year 2000 – perhaps by as much as 120 million. Use of the appellation 'Second World' to describe the socialist realm is arguably more appropriate than use of 'Third World' to describe developing countries. This is largely because of the ideological restrictions on links between socialist states and the west and the corresponding emphasis upon developing economic, social, and political ties among socialist states themselves. COMECON, a mutual economic alliance between the states of eastern Europe and the USSR, affords one of the clearest examples of such ties. As some parts of this book reveal, however, the Second World is far from being totally disengaged from the capitalist realm. The USSR exports oil and natural gas to the west and buys grain to make up harvest deficits in return. Manufactured goods from eastern Europe are becoming a steadily more familiar sight in the shops of western Europe, a function of lower production costs and a growing range of trade agreements. Western firms now manufacture under licence in some socialist states, while western banks and financial institutions have become an increasing source of credit in the face of accumulating trade imbalances occasioned by much-needed imports of food and other consumables. The sections of this book which deal with trade make clear that the scale of east–west trade is exceedingly limited relative to the scale of trade among states of the west. But as the socialist realm is increasingly beset with new internal problems and as more 'open-door' policies prevail, the context for extended trade relations will likely widen.

One of the major difficulties in compiling a book of this kind is that it is forever running out-of-date. And this problem is compounded by the time it takes for organizations like the UN to collect, process, and publish data. Thus, even with the most recent published material to hand, one is invariably two to three years out of phase. A more profound difficulty arises from the permanent state of flux of the capitalist system.[15] The direction of change is never certain and often dubious. And events like the world stockmarket crash of October 1987 demonstrate forcefully the system's capacity for sudden crisis; shock-waves were registered throughout the entire free world.[16] In this sense, some of the trends revealed in this book can be only the most partial of guides to the course of change or of evolution. Added to this, moreover, there is the growing realization of environmental degradation, particularly to the earth's atmosphere. In other words, the future may hold an altogether different kind of crisis, the mechanisms of which will likely be even more imperfectly understood than those of capitalism.

Michael Freeman, Oxford, March 1989

Notes and references

1 The substance of the World Bank's approach can be seen in its *World Development Report*, published annually by Oxford University Press. Whatever deficiencies one may claim to find in the reports, they remain a formidable

source of contemporary statistical material on the capitalist world; they also contain much important economic commentary on the developing world

2 For further general discussion, see H. R. Jones *A Population Geography* pp. 130–1 (London, 1981); R. I. Woods *Population Analysis in Geography,* pp. 17–18 (London, 1979)

3 For example, in passenger-car production for 1983, the UN gives France and Sweden as manufacturing 3,228,000 and 281,000 units respectively (*UN Statistical Yearbook,* New York, 1983–4), whereas the Society of Motor Manufacturers and Traders of GB gives parallel figures of 2,960,823 and 344,702 in its international summary table (*The Motor Industry of Great Britain,* London, 1987). In world iron-ore production, the *Metal Bulletin Handbook,* vol. 2 (Worcester Park, England, 1985) gives an output figure for 1981 of 847,782,000 tonnes, whereas the *Metal Bulletin's Prices and Data* (Worcester Park, England, 1987) gives a parallel figure of 884,866,000 tonnes. In neither of these particular examples are we dealing with small discrepancies; nor are there immediately obvious explanations for them

4 In some production areas, actual annual production figures can be found freely available. This applies, for example, in Soviet iron and steel manufacture – see *Metal Bulletin Handbook,* vol. 2 (1985). From the same source, however, Soviet aluminium production for 1981–3 is recorded as 2.4 million tonnes annually

5 It is, for example, exceptionally difficult to calculate GNP per capita statistics for non-market economies

6 All of these features, as well as others, are addressed in the *UN Demographic Yearbook*

7 For further discussion of some of these issues, see D. Grigg, *The World Food Problem,* pp. 73–9 (Oxford, 1985)

8 See, for instance, D. G. Dalrymple, *Development and Spread of High Yielding Varieties of Wheat and Rice in Less Developed Nations* (Washington, 1978)

9 See M. Davis, 'Chinatown, Part Two? The "Internationalization of Downtown Los Angeles"', *New Left Review* 149 (1987) 65–84

10 Some of these aspects are treated in L. Timberlake *Africa in Crisis: The Causes, the Cures of Environmental Bankruptcy* (London, 1988)

11 See B. Snowdon, 'The political economy of the Ethiopian famine', *National Westminster Bank Quarterly Review* (1985) pp. 41–55

12 See Timberlake, op. cit.

13 See, for example, P. Richards, *Indigenous Agricultural Revolution: Ecology and Food Production in West Africa* (London, 1985)

14 See A. J. Jowett (1984) 'The growth of China's population, 1949–1982', *Geographical Journal* 150, (1984) pp. 155–70

15 See, for example, D. Harvey 'Changing the geography of geographical change', *Geography Review* 2 (1988) pp. 2–4

16 See D. Harvey 'The hurricane in stock markets' (editorial), *Geography Review* 1 (1987)

Burmese refugees in northern Thailand

1
Population

The world's growing millions

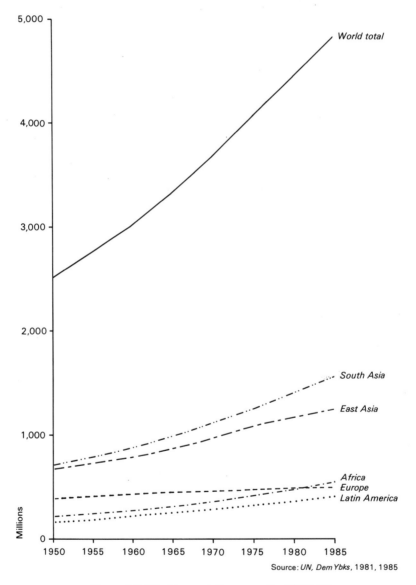

Figure 1.1 World population growth, 1950–85

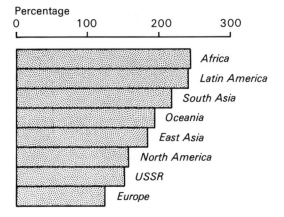

Figure 1.2 Percentage growth in population, 1950–85

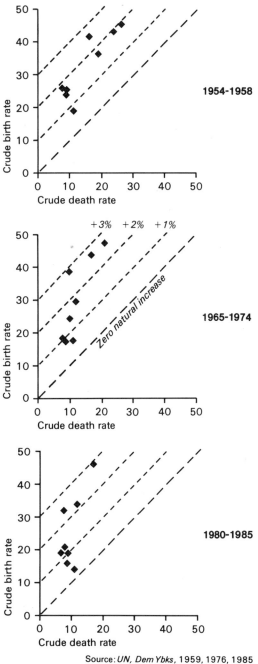

The growth of the human population has been one of the most spectacular aspects of the world economy in the third quarter of the twentieth century. Between 1950 and 1985, in fact, the world's population almost doubled, and this led many commentators to forecast a new Malthusian crisis in the twenty-first century. Phrases such as 'teeming millions', 'standing room only' and 'ecocatastrophe' pervaded the literature. But for some years now there have been clear indications of a slowing down in the rate of growth. Whereas over 1960–70 the level was 2.23 per cent, in 1970–80 it fell to 2.05 and in the half-decade 1980–5 to 1.74. The trends in vital rates, as depicted in Figure 1.3, afford some illustration of the pattern. None of this is to say that there are no population problems in the world. It is simply to place a question-mark over the ever-strengthening exponential curve upon which so many world forecasts have traditionally been made. In the 1980s, population forecasts for the twenty-first century have been distinguished for their continuing *downward* revisions.

Source: *UN, Dem Ybks*, 1959, 1976, 1985

Figure 1.3 Vital rates in the major regions of the world

The regional dimension

Easily the most startling feature of modern world population growth has been its spatial divergence. Annual rates of growth at a continental scale currently vary from 2.9 per cent in Africa to 0.3 per cent in Europe. At subcontinental scales, western and northern Europe show rates of 0.1 per cent, while western and eastern Africa show 3.1 per cent. The effect of such differentials over time has been to produce a remarkable shift in the geographical balance of the world's population.

In 1950, for instance, Africa had only 8.9 per cent of the world's population; in 1985 it had 11.5 per cent. The corresponding figures for South Asia were 28.0 per cent and 32.4 per cent, giving that major world region one third of the entire world population by the mid-1980s. Europe, by contrast, has seen its share fall from 15.6 per cent to 10.2 per cent. The USSR and North America also recorded decreased shares.

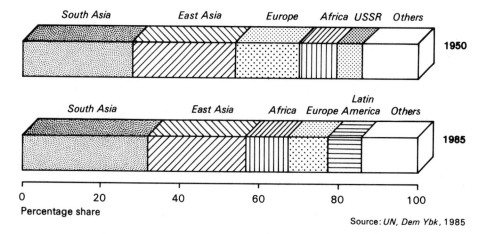

Source: UN, Dem Ybk, 1985

Figure 1.4 Regional shares of the world population

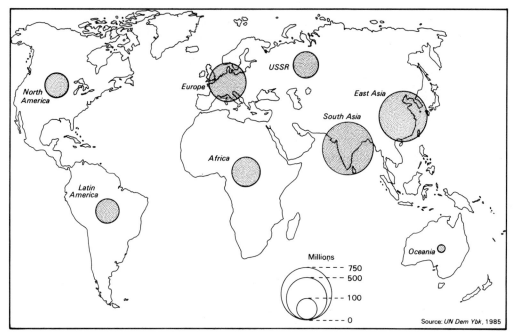

Figure 1.5 World population in 1950

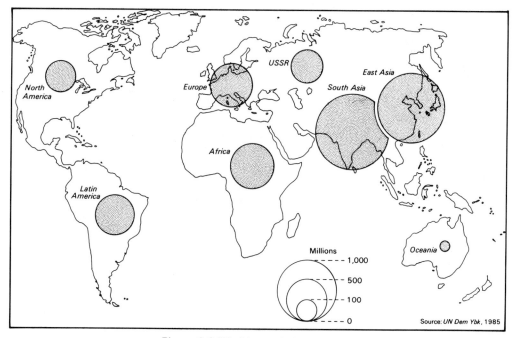

Figure 1.6 World population in 1985

Population by state

The dominating shares of East and South Asia in world population are yet more clearly highlighted when one examines the populations of individual states. Figure 1.7 depicts the estimated totals for the world's states in mid-1986. The massive scale of the Chinese and Indian populations relative to those of other nation-states is immediately apparent. Naturally, one may argue that such a map produces a distorted picture of the geographical balance of world population because the areas of nation-states vary greatly in size:

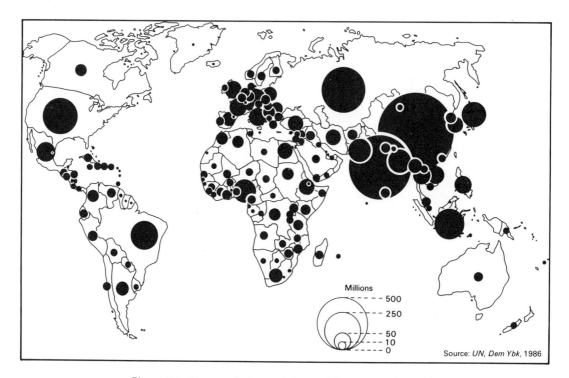

Figure 1.7 The populations of the world's states, mid-1986

were there, for example, a 'United States of Europe', the western hemisphere would be much more prominent. However, the merits of such an approach to world population are many. In the case of the African continent, for instance, population is concentrated in a small number of states; and this is a feature which is little compromised by the particular geographical division of the continent: there are, so to speak, no 'Chinas' in Africa. The nation-state may also have importance for the dynamics of population: indirectly via economic structure or policy, or more directly through a society's cultural values, including deliberate population control by the apparatus of the state. China made birth control a national policy from 1971 and by 1980 most municipalities and provinces had established incentives and disincentives to promote 'one-child' families.

The scale of absolute increases in national populations between 1960 and mid-1986 is shown in Figure 1.8. Over this 27-year period, the world's population grew by some 2 billion. And the contribution of South and East Asia to that expansion is inescapably evident. The west, including Europe and North America, pales into insignificance by comparison. It remains true, though, that in much of South and East Asia, environments are capable of supporting high densities of population, notwithstanding the problems posed by climatic or other instabilities. In Africa, by contrast, optimum densities are exceptionally low in all but a limited number of areas, and the scale of population growth is fast approaching them, if not already in breach in certain cases. As later pages will show, it is in Africa, above all, that fears about Malthusian catastrophes are at their most real.

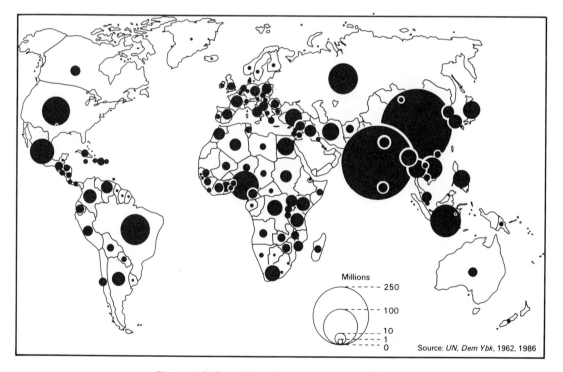

Figure 1.8 Population increase by state, 1960–86

Population structure

One of the primary reasons why continents like Africa and Asia show such high rates of population increase lies in population age structure. Most countries in these areas have what are called 'youthful' populations, with relatively high proportions in the reproductive age-group. In Africa in 1985, some 45 per cent of its population were under 15 years, presenting a formidable base for population expansion into the twenty-first century unless checked by moral or government-imposed restraint, or by 'Malthusian' controls. The contrast is with Europe, where only 21 per cent of the population were under 15 years in 1985 and where 25 per cent were 65 years or over. The 'ageing' structure of some European populations has meant that they have begun registering death rates which are actually higher than the levels in some developing countries. In northern Europe in 1985, for instance, the rate was 12 per thousand, whereas the rate for all parts of Latin America, for example, was only 8. Such low levels of

death rates, when combined with high birth rates, naturally form the ingredients of explosive population growth. In the graph of vital rates for Asia over 1980–5 (Figure 1.10), it is clear that many states recorded death rates below 10 per thousand, but still maintained birth rates of 20 per thousand upwards. African states show a higher average death rate than in Asia (17 as against 10), but this is more than compensated by a much higher average birth rate (46 against 27), giving a rate of natural increase in 1980–5 of 2.9 per cent per annum compared with 1.7 per cent for Asia. Africa is the one area of the world where 'crisis' is a description which accurately reflects the conditions of population expansion. Current projections suggest a population of 900 million by the year 2000; in 1985 the figure was 555 million. Already food supply per capita is following a downward trend in Africa. The prognosis, in other words, cannot be anything but grim.

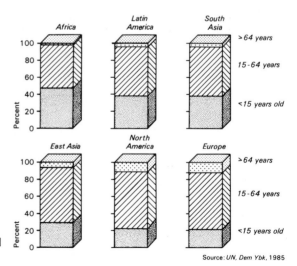

Figure 1.9 Age structures of major world populations, 1985

Source: *UN, Dem Ybk*, 1985

16

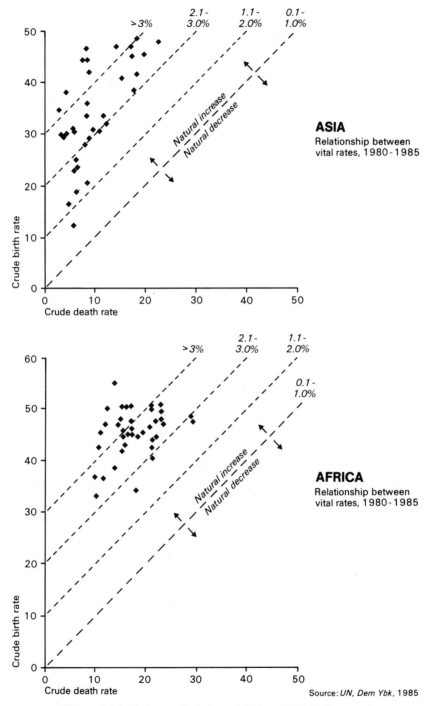

Source: *UN, Dem Ybk*, 1985

Figure 1.10 Vital rates in Asia and Africa, 1980–5 (by state)

Asian population

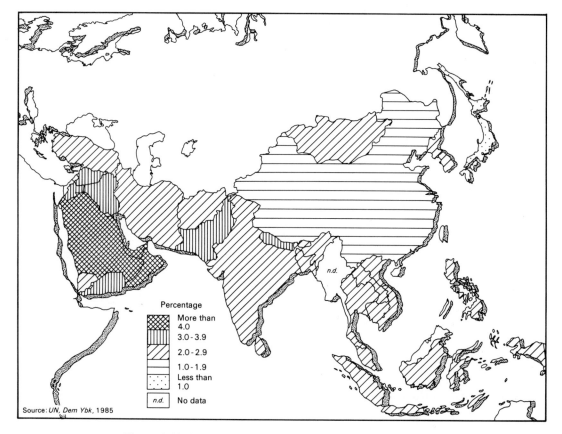

Figure 1.11 Asia: annual rate of population increase, 1980–5

Excluding the Soviet Union, the Asian continent in 1980–5 recorded a rate of population increase of 1.7 per cent (exactly the world average, in fact). Predictably, though, this figure hides a wide variation between states. For instance, the Arab states of Qatar and UAR recorded 6.9 and 6.2 per cent respectively in 1980–5, while Japan recorded only 0.7. Already with 120 million people on their islands in 1985, the Japanese have every incentive to pursue such a low rate of increase. But for Qatar and the UAR, their populations are so small that apparently excessive rates of growth signify relatively little. When rates of growth are related to base population, the focus inevitably moves to China and India. In 1985 the People's Republic had an estimated 1.06 billion people, while India had 0.75 billion. In the mid-1960s, the divergence between birth and death rates in China was of the order of 30 per thousand, giving a natural increase of 3 per cent per annum. When projected to the year 2000, this gave a population approaching or above two billion and prompted renewed government efforts to lower the birth rate by persuasion and coercion. The effects of China's famous 'one-child policy' are clearly apparent in Figure 1.12. The CBR had dropped to just below 20 by 1980 and for 1980–5 the estimated rate of natural increase was 1.2 per cent.

In India, the world's largest democracy, there has been little parallel to the birth-control achievements in neighbouring China. Without central economic planning and without the powerful bureaucracy of the state machine, India has had to fall back upon persuasive measures and on the autonomous forces of economic and social modernization. Indeed, when the Indian government in the mid-1970s sought to pursue a rigorous sterilization policy, the results were poor, as well as politically destabilizing. Hence India retains a high rate of natural increase (2.5 per cent), although not without considerable areal/regional diversity. In the 1950s, the crude birth rate averaged 44 per thousand. By the 1980s it was still around 34.

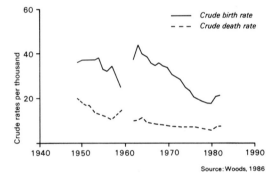

Source: Woods, 1986

Figure 1.12 China: changes in estimated vital rates, 1950–85

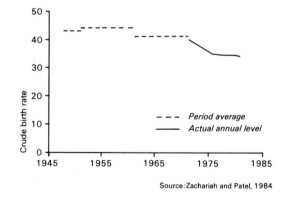

Source: Zachariah and Patel, 1984

Figure 1.13 India: fertility, 1948–81

African population

Analysis of the demographic characteristics of Africa, both now and in the recent past, must begin by stressing the difficulties of obtaining accurate and reliable data. Thus in the map of fertility trends, 1962–5 to 1980–5 (Figure 1.15), the category 'no change' has been applied to states recording changes of up to plus or minus 2 per thousand. Taking Africa as a whole, fertility fell by roughly 2 per thou-

sand over these two decades, from 48 to 46 per thousand. In the world, the corresponding reduction was roughly 7 per thousand. Only 3 out of the 47 African states matched this world scale of decline: Algeria, Morocco, and Tunisia. Most states showed static or near-static levels, while some, like Uganda and Tanzania, showed decisive gains.

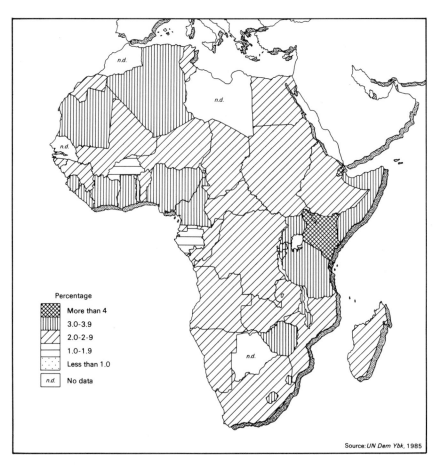

Figure 1.14 Africa: annual rate of population increase, 1980–5

If the time-scale is extended backwards, it becomes apparent that African fertility levels at large have signally failed to respond to the various modernizing forces which have affected the continent in the decades since 1950. The estimated crude birth rate in 1950–5 was 48 per thousand, so that in 30 years it has fallen back by only 2. When levels of the crude death rate are examined, however, the impact of modernization, in particular the export by the west of its methods of 'death control', is hard to escape. Between 1962–5 and 1980–5, the rate for Africa as a whole fell from roughly 25 to 17. Since about 1960, therefore, while average birth rates have

declined by less than 1 per thousand in every ten years, average death rates have fallen by over 3 per thousand. The inevitable corollary has been a startling acceleration in population growth, heavily concentrated in the states of East and West Africa, where some 60 per cent of the continent's population is to be found. Nigeria, the most populous state of Africa (95 million), had a rate of natural increase of 3.4 per cent per annum over 1980–5, deriving from a crude birth rate of 50/51 and a crude death rate of 17. But Kenya, though less populated (20.3 million), surpassed this with a rate of increase of 4.1, deriving from birth and death rates of 55 and 14 respectively.

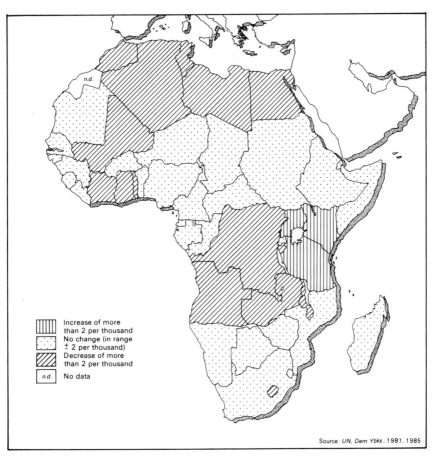

Figure 1.15 Africa: fertility trends, 1962–5 to 1980–5

European population

Europe is the continental area of the world where population is to be found in the most stable of conditions. With the exception of Albania, no country now shows a natural increase greater than 1 per cent per annum. Most are recording levels of below 0.5; and not a few are exhibiting natural decrease. The latter phenomenon seems certain to increase in incidence as the impact of the falling birth rate of the most recent decades feeds through to the reproductive generation and as the proportions of the population aged 65 and over grow. The phenomenon of the 'ageing population' is increasingly common among European states, presenting serious problems for their governments in the maintenance of social welfare. Substantial annual increases in budgetary allocations for health and welfare services are necessary just to maintain existing levels of provision per capita of population. The concept of 'zero growth', in other words, is not quite such a desirable population condition after all.

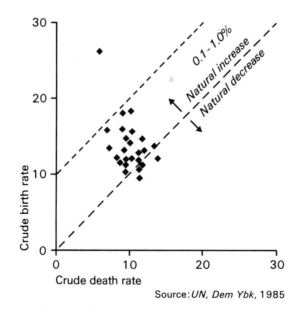

Source: *UN, Dem Ybk*, 1985

Figure 1.16 Europe: vital rates, 1980–5

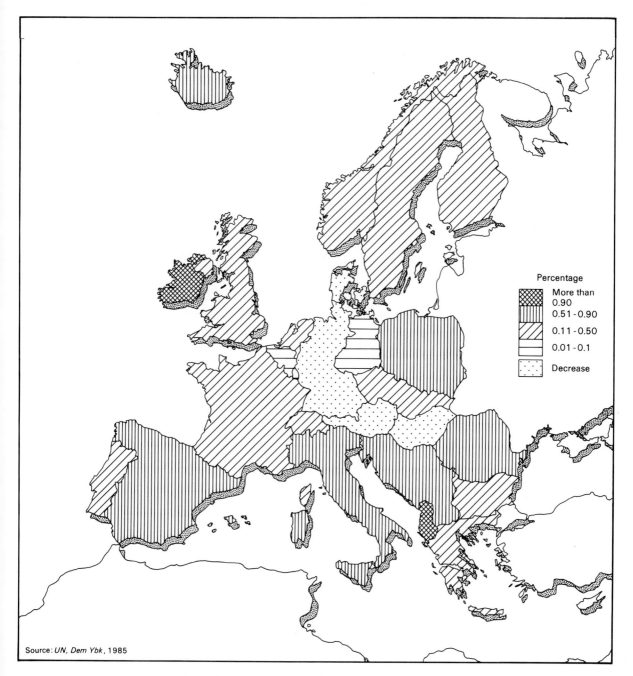

Source: *UN, Dem Ybk*, 1985

Figure 1.17 Europe: rates of natural increase, 1980–5

Population 'urban'

Figure 1.18 Africa: urban
population, early 1980s

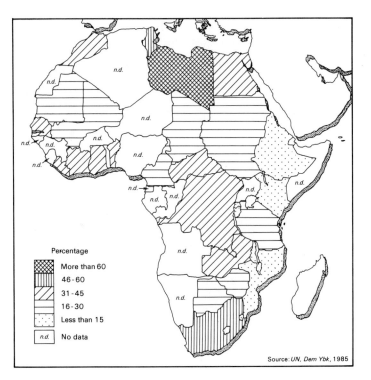

Percentage

More than 60
46-60
31-45
16-30
Less than 15
n.d. No data

Source: *UN, Dem Ybk*, 1985

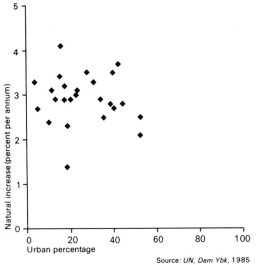

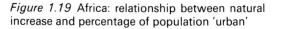
Source: *UN, Dem Ybk*, 1985

Figure 1.19 Africa: relationship between natural
increase and percentage of population 'urban'

24

It is commonplace to view the degree of urbanization in a country as a rough index of the degree of modernization. The idea springs from the experience of Britain and various other western nations as they industrialized over the course of the nineteenth century. In the United Kingdom today, 87.7 per cent of the population is classed as urban. In Belgium it is 94.6 per cent. But this is a relationship that does not carry too wide a currency. Peru, for example, has 68.9 per cent of its population classed as urban, Chile 83.2 per cent. And yet neither country can be considered to have been 'modernized' to the extent of western European nations. The broad thesis may be tested further in Africa. One might reasonably posit that levels of urbanization and rates of natural increase of population are inversely correlated. In reality, there is only the barest of such relationships, as Figure 1.19 demonstrates. If one focuses on the continents of South America and Asia, the confusion grows. In the former case, most countries are classed as more than 60 per cent urbanized, but Asia shows an average of less than half this figure. China, for example, had only about one-fifth

of its population classed as urban in the early 1980s. It would undoubtedly be a mistake to deny that urbanization and modernization are related themes. But there are other variables to be considered. First, there is no universal definition of what is 'urban'. Hence, the figures mapped on these pages differ, in some measure, because of varying national census designs. A number of writers have used this as an argument to exclude international comparisons in the level of urbanization, but this is inappropriate. Although the precise instruments of measurement may vary, there is a general consensus which sees urban as relating to non-agricultural populations. Other variables which require consideration are settlement history, terrain (including agricultural potential), and the prevailing form of political economy. South American states, for example, show high urbanization levels partly because of their colonial and settlement histories. In China, by comparison, the combination of intensive-farming potential and the structure of the rural commune have made for a correspondingly low level.

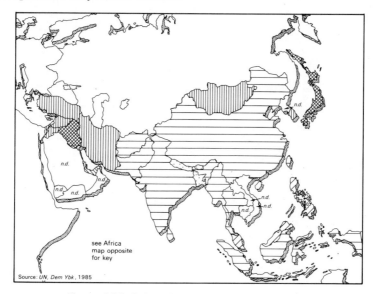

Figure 1.20 Asia: urban population, early 1980s

25

Prairie farming in Oxfordshire, United Kingdom

2
Agriculture

Food supply and population

The primary foodgrains

Cropped area, productivity, and food composition

Food supply and population in developing countries:
the crisis in Africa

Food supply and population in developing countries:
South and East Asia

Factors of production

Agriculture in the economy

The grain trade

Food supply and population

Contrary to many popular perceptions, there has been consistent growth in average per-capita food supply in the world since 1950. Thus the proportions of the populations of the developed and developing worlds receiving less than the basic metabolic rate fell from 13 and 34 per cent respectively in 1948–50 to 12 and 17 per cent in 1978–80. But when percentages are translated back into absolute numbers and when averages are related back to their underlying statistical distributions, it becomes clear why the problem of hunger remains such a potent one. For example, in 1978–80, as in 1948–50, there were still half a billion people in the developing world receiving less than the basic metabolic rate. And in Africa, some countries show huge shortfalls in minimum nutrition levels: the so-called 'calorie gap'.

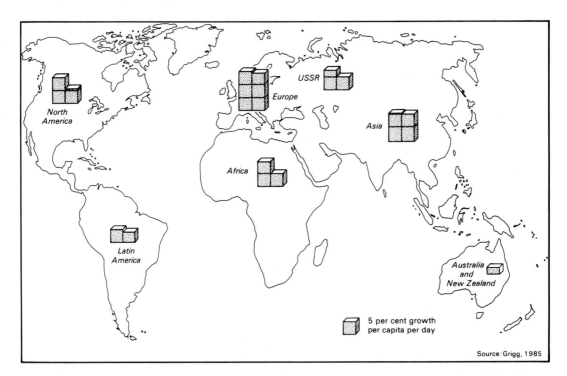

Figure 2.1 Percentage growth in average available food supply per capita per day, 1950–80

Figure 2.2 expresses the available calorie supply per capita per day as a percentage of the minimum requirements set on a country-by-country basis in the Fourth World Food Survey of 1977. Africa is undeniably the most serious area of deficient nutrition in the world, although its countries display a wide range of conditions and any single country may well show substantial variation within its borders. On past trends, Ethiopia and Chad (no data here) would have shared much the same experience as their neighbours, making vast tracts of Africa south of the Sahara subject to deficient nutrition.

Most recent trends in food production reveal that Africa is in decline, reaching a major trough in 1983 and 1984. By contrast, in the planned economies of Asia the production trend has been vigorously upward. And for the world as a whole, there appears little sign of faltering in the advance of production.

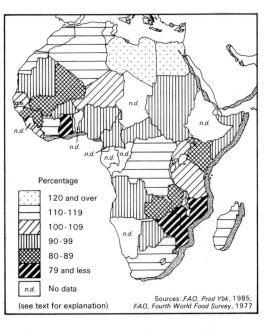

Figure 2.2 Africa: the calorie gap, 1981–3

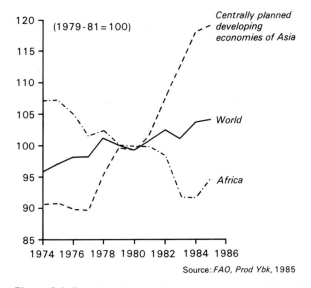

Figure 2.3 Food production indices per capita, 1974–85

The primary foodgrains

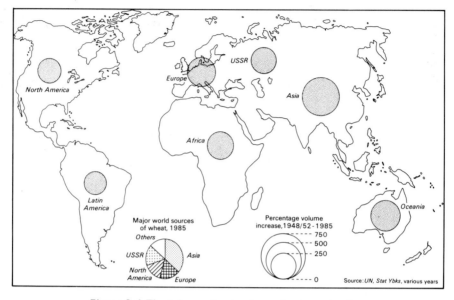

Figure 2.4 The primary foodgrains: wheat production

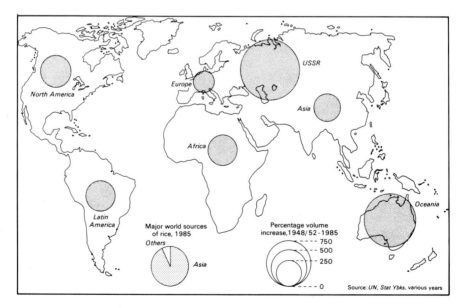

Figure 2.5 The primary foodgrains: rice production

Around 1980, wheat, rice, and maize accounted for some 80 per cent of all cereals produced in the world. Figure 2.6 shows a remarkably strong upward trend in the production of all three grains, especially since 1965. Asia dominates in rice and wheat, North America in maize. In 1950 Asia was ranked only third in the world production of wheat. Since then it has ousted both North America and Europe. A primary factor in the expansion of wheat output in Asia has been the introduction of high-yielding varieties. In Asia (excluding China) nearly three-quarters of the sown-wheat area was under HYVs in 1976–7.

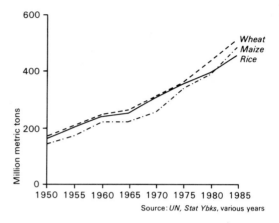

Figure 2.6 World production of major cereals, 1950–85

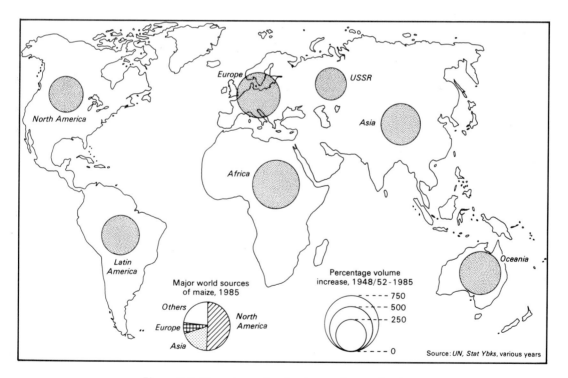

Figure 2.7 The primary foodgrains: maize production

31

Cropped area, productivity, and food composition

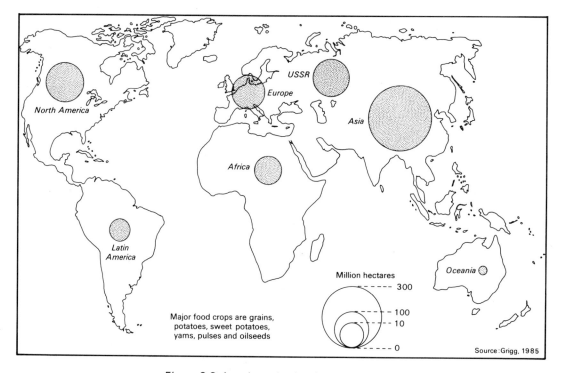

Figure 2.8 Area in major foodcrops, 1948–52

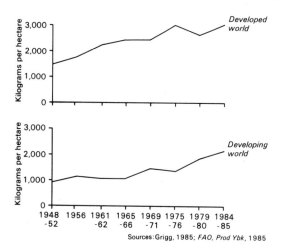

Figure 2.9 Yield of cereals, 1950–85

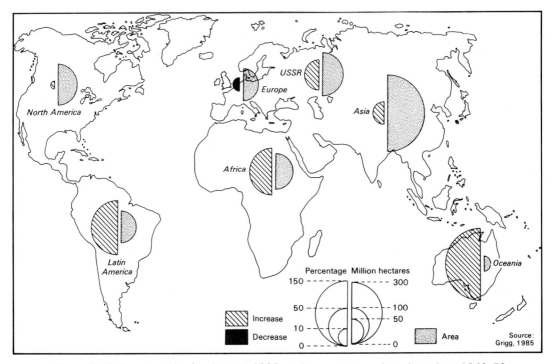

Figure 2.10 Area in major food crops, 1980, and percentage gain or loss since 1948–52

The area of the world under major food crops (grains, potatoes, sweet potatoes, yams, pulses, and oilseeds) grew by almost a quarter between 1948–52 and 1980, and by nearly a third in the developing world alone. Cereal yields in the developed world doubled over the same time-span; in the developing world the scale of advance was 125 per cent, much of it recorded from the mid-1970s. The relative contributions of area extension and yield improvement to growth in cereal output, 1950–80, were 3:97 in the developed world and 40:60 in the developing world.

The composition of recent world food production is illustrated in Figure 2.11. Non-cereal output in this case includes root-crops, pulses, fruit and vegetables, nuts, sugar, meat, milk, and eggs. It is not advisable to take this ratio too much at face value, for nutritional values vary between different foodstuffs. There is also the problem that some items of

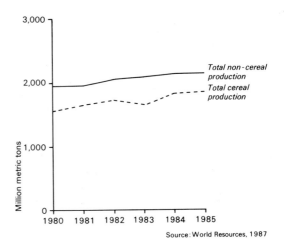

Figure 2.11 World food production, 1980–5

output are used as animal feed. Nevertheless, the literal force of the term 'foodgrain' is inescapable.

33

Food supply and population in developing countries: the crisis in Africa

The problems of African food supply stand out even more vividly in Figure 2.12. Over a very large portion of the continental area, food production has failed to keep abreast of population growth. In Botswana, Mozambique, and Guinea-Bissau, moreover, population growth rates of 3.6 per cent and above were accompanied by a percentage *decrease* in food output. For energy-exporting states like Algeria, Libya, and Nigeria, the weaknesses are more apparent than real. Elsewhere in Africa, though, nothing could be further from the truth. And circumstances have been made worse by drought and by civil strife, and by the refugee problems which have inevitably arisen in their wake. As Figure 2.13 shows, over the period 1977 to 1984 there were thirteen states affected by recurrent food shortages according to the UN's Food and Agriculture Organization. Most had experienced abnormal climatic conditions.

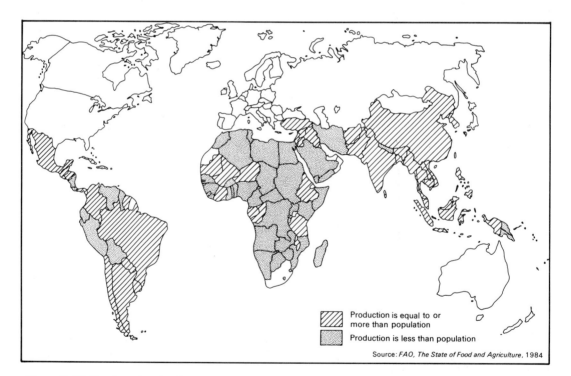

Production is equal to or more than population

Production is less than population

Source: *FAO, The State of Food and Agriculture, 1984*

Figure 2.12 Food production in relation to population growth, 1974–84, in 105 developing countries

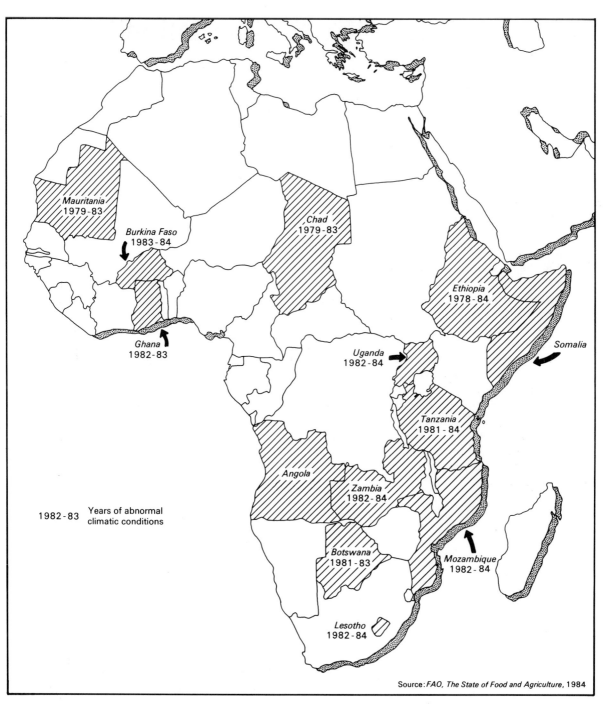

Mauritania
1979 - 83

Burkina Faso
1983 - 84

Chad
1979 - 83

Ethiopia
1978 - 84

Ghana
1982 - 83

Somalia

Uganda
1982 - 84

Tanzania
1981 - 84

1982 - 83   Years of abnormal
             climatic conditions

Angola

Zambia
1982 - 84

Botswana
1981 - 83

Mozambique
1982 - 84

Lesotho
1982 - 84

Source: *FAO, The State of Food and Agriculture*, 1984

Figure 2.13 Africa: countries recurrently affected by food shortages, 1977–84

Food supply and population in developing countries: South and East Asia

Of all the continental regions of the developing world, Asia, or South and East Asia, stands out as the most successful in keeping food production abreast of population growth. In India, as Figure 2.14 reveals, the level of per-capita cereal production has shown a fairly consistent upward trend from 1950 to the mid-1980s. Moreover, during the later 1970s and early 1980s, when Africa was experiencing a sharp deterioration in its agricultural position, India, along with most other Asian states, was recording almost continuous improvement – as witnessed, for example, in the growth of cereal yields between 1974 and 1985 (see Figure 2.15).

One of the striking features of Indian cereal production is the relative absence of any decisive upturn in the wake of the so-called 'Green Revolution' from the mid-1960s. Spectacular advances in yields (in wheat especially) were certainly recorded in some areas of northern India, but the popular image of the HYV programme as having forged a widespread and lasting revolution in production and productivity is largely a fiction. HYV technology has simply been one of a range of components of Indian agricultural improvement operating over varying time-scales and in varying geographical settings.

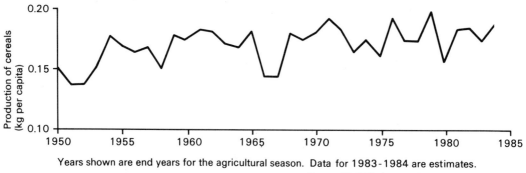

Years shown are end years for the agricultural season. Data for 1983-1984 are estimates.

Source: World Bank, *World Development Report*, 1984

Figure 2.14 India: cereal production, 1950–84

36

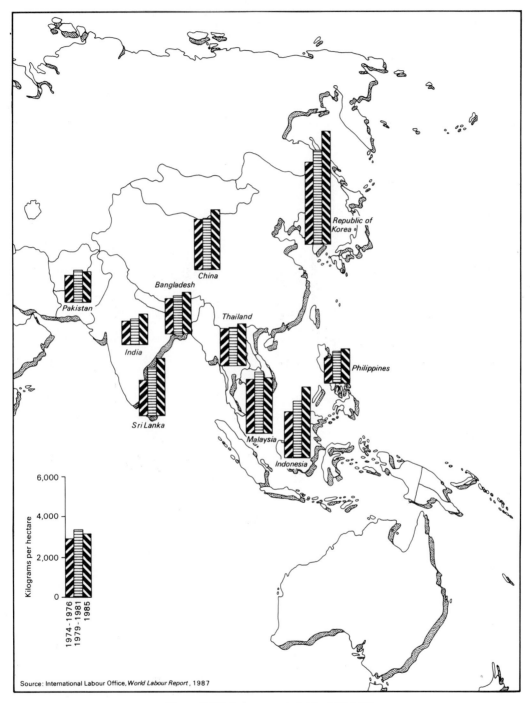

Source: International Labour Office, *World Labour Report*, 1987

Figure 2.15 Asia: cereal yields, 1974–85

Factors of production

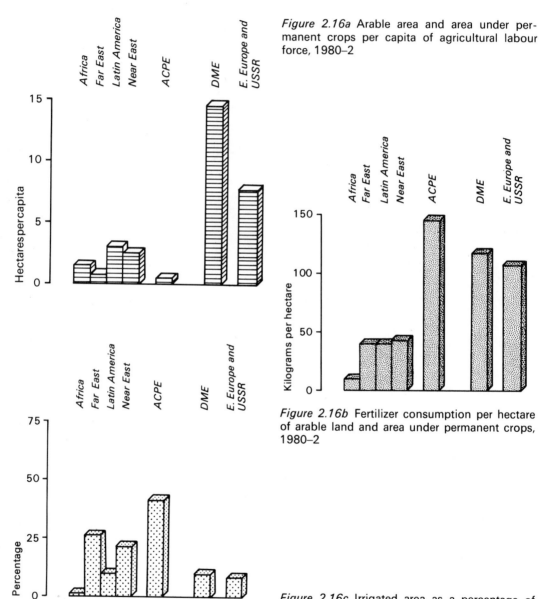

Figure 2.16a Arable area and area under permanent crops per capita of agricultural labour force, 1980–2

Figure 2.16b Fertilizer consumption per hectare of arable land and area under permanent crops, 1980–2

Figure 2.16c Irrigated area as a percentage of arable land and area under permanent crops, 1980–2

Source: *FAO, The State of Food and Agriculture*, 1985

38

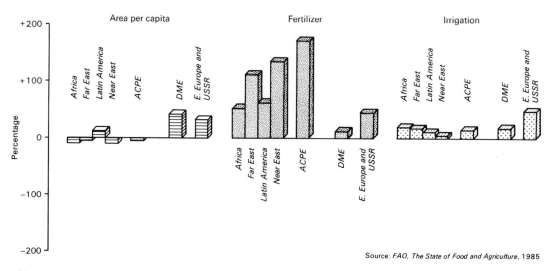

Source: *FAO, The State of Food and Agriculture*, 1985

Figure 2.17 Change in cultivated area per capita, fertilizer consumption, and irrigated area, 1971–3 to 1980–2

The ingredients of an advancing per-capita food supply cannot be rationalized in any simple or universal manner. The attainments of the centrally planned economies of Asia (ACPE – which comprises China, Kampuchea, Democratic People's Republic of Korea, Mongolia, and Vietnam) since about 1970 afford illustration of this: while cultivated land area per capita of the farm workforce has declined by 22.6 per cent, per-capita food production has raced forward. In the developed market economies of the west (DME), production advances of this sort have typically been achieved against the backcloth of increasing ratios of land to workers, not declining ones.

The apparent capacity of small peasant holdings to yield major production gains has to be set alongside a vast leap in fertilizer use in the ACPE. In 1980–2, application levels were higher than in the DME, having grown by some 172 per cent over the preceding decade. Irrigation levels were also higher in the ACPE in 1980–2 than elsewhere, although the pace of irrigation extension after 1970 was slow.

Agriculture in the economy

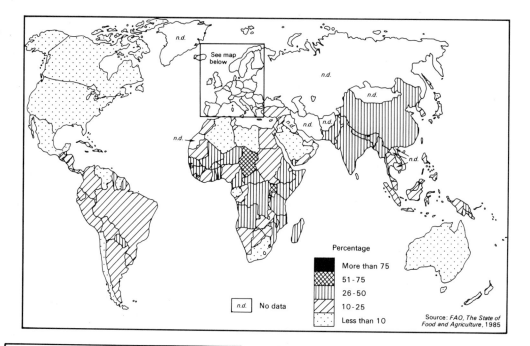

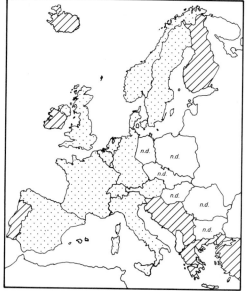

Figure 2.18 Agricultural GDP as a percentage of total GDP, 1982

For most countries of the developed world, agriculture's contribution to gross domestic product is very low, and has been so for much of the post-war period. The paradox, though, is that it is some of these very countries which produce the bulk of the world's food surplus for trade with food-deficit nations. Canada, France, and the United States are three primary cases in point. Countries in which agriculture contributes very substantially to GDP are concentrated in Africa and South/Southeast Asia. For many of these countries, too, agricultural goods provide the bulk of exports. In 1984, in Africa as a whole, the

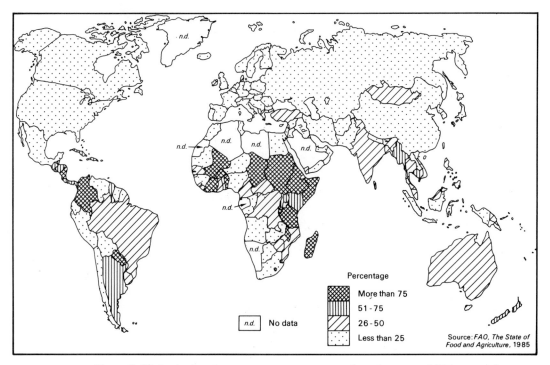

Figure 2.19 Agricultural exports as a percentage of total exports, 1984

	1965	1985
Africa	73.5	62.2
South America	42.0	24.9
Asia	71.8	62.1
North Central America	17.8	14.0
Europe	23.7	11.3
Oceania	22.8	18.5

Source: FAO, Prod Ybk, 1985

Figure 2.20 Agricultural population as a percentage of total population

figure was 49 per cent. Familiar plantation crops like tea and coffee dominate this pattern, often resulting in the need to import foodstuffs to sustain the indigenous population. Such export crops have proven highly volatile income-earners, sometimes with very unsatisfactory results for national well-being.

The varying contributions of agriculture to GDP across the world are reflected in the percentages of the population deriving their livelihoods directly from agriculture. Both Africa and Asia, for example, still have mainly two-thirds of their populations so dependent. In all continental areas of the world, the scale of this ratio has contracted since the mid-1960s, which leaves one to question how cultivated land area per capita has remained static or even declined in many parts. The answer, of course, lies in the absolute statistics of population growth.

The grain trade

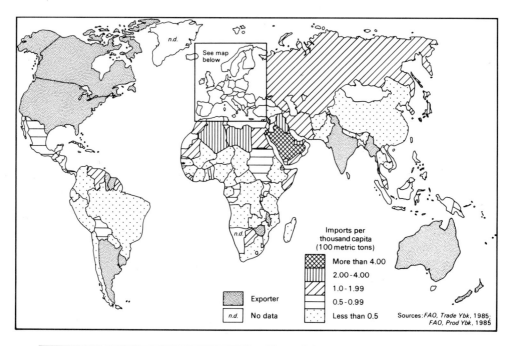

Imports per
thousand capita
(100 metric tons)

More than 4.00
2.00 - 4.00
1.0 - 1.99
0.5 - 0.99
Less than 0.5

Exporter

n.d. No data

Sources: FAO, Trade Ybk, 1985;
FAO, Prod Ybk, 1985

Figure 2.21 Net grain importers, 1985

Sources: Grigg, 1985; *FAO, Trade Ybk*, 1985

Figure 2.22 World grain trade, 1950–85

World trade in foodgrains or cereals has grown dramatically since 1950, with the continent of North America emerging as the undisputed breadbasket of the world. Over the years 1950 to 1980, North American grain exports quadrupled. Africa, the USSR and its eastern European satellites, and Asia have emerged as the leading importers, in ascending order of importance. Asian imports were almost negligible around 1950, but by 1985 they had reached nearly 60 million metric tons. Large-scale imports should not necessarily be perceived as a sign of weakness, either at a continental or at a national level. The fact that the highest per-capita grain importer in 1985 was Saudi Arabia offers demonstration of this. Indeed, in the case of African countries, it would be relatively easy to argue that high scales of per-capita grain imports indicate high scales of national income. And the corollary is quite well represented in the way much of sub-Saharan Africa occupies the lowest league in the import stakes (see Figure 2.21). This cannot be a universal rule of thumb, of course. China, for instance, cannot be viewed in this manner. But in zones of long-standing and intractable deficit in agricultural potential, the pattern is a valid one.

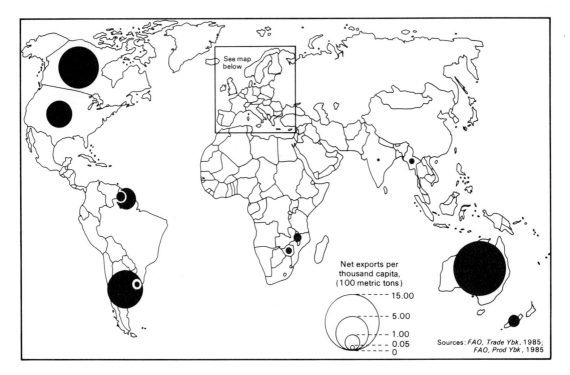

Figure 2.23 Net grain exporters, 1985

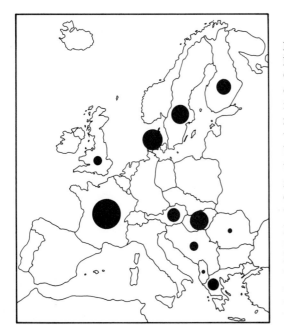

Reports of huge North American grain surpluses and of 'grain mountains' in the European Community are viewed by many as a classic failing of the capitalist mode of production in the supply of food to mankind. It is essential to remember, however, that some measure of stockpiling is necessary given the vagaries of nature; in fact, insurance against bad harvest years was a feature of some of the earliest agricultural societies. The more germane question concerns the necessary *scale* of retained surpluses. By the early 1980s, these were running at 250–300 million metric tons per annum, or 15–20 per cent of total consumption, roughly two-thirds of them in the hands of regular grain exporters. Such a volume figure appears excessive when it is established that the USA and Canada, together forming by far the largest export block, traded only 100 million metric tons in

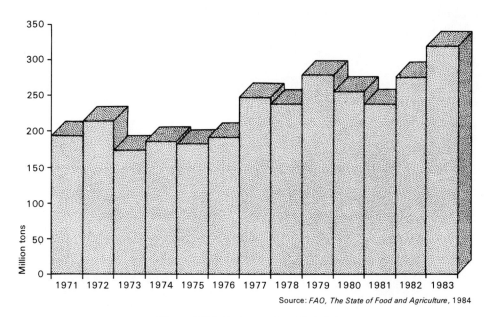

Source: *FAO, The State of Food and Agriculture*, 1984

Figure 2.24 Grain stocks, 1971–83

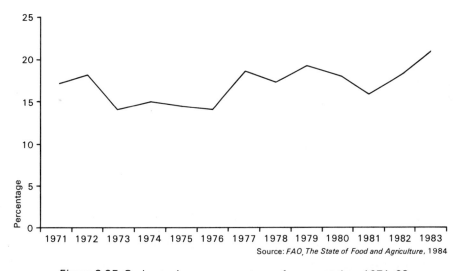

Source: *FAO, The State of Food and Agriculture*, 1984

Figure 2.25 Grain stocks as a percentage of consumption, 1971–83

1985. A yet more salutary statistic is the volume of cereals shipped as food aid – a mere 10 million metric tons in the early 1980s. The UN Food and Agriculture Organization reckons that the minimum security level for stocks is 17–18 per cent of apparent consumption in any one year. However, the rationale behind so precise a figure is unclear.

Cooling towers at Didcot coal-fired power station, Oxfordshire, United Kingdom

3
Energy

Energy use

Over the course of the twentieth century, a rising level of energy use has been increasingly perceived as a vital hallmark of development and progress. At times, in fact, energy consumption per capita almost appears to have acquired the status of an independent variable, against which developments in other fields like communications are measured and evaluated. The extension of industrialization to many different countries of the world, especially since 1945, offers one explanation for the trend, as does the emergence of more advanced industrial societies with their burgeoning demands for consumer durables. Beyond this, however, it is vital to register the declining costs of energy, notably since the Second World War. The growth of competing energy resources has contributed to this, as

have developments in the production scale and production organization of energy sectors like oil. The outcome of these various forces is depicted in Figure 3.1. In particular, it demonstrates the sharp acceleration in the rate of energy use from the early 1940s which led commentators to talk so readily of a neo-Malthusian resource crisis by the turn of the millennium. As the graph indicates, though, there has been a correspondingly sharp deceleration in the rate of energy use in the 1970s and early 1980s. Major downturns in the world capitalist economy have contributed to the change. The growth of the 'environmental lobby' has promoted greater efficiency in energy use. However, the prime catalyst has been the alteration in the oil market.

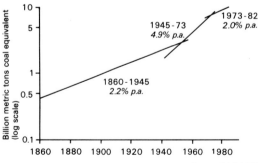

Source : Odell, 1986   *Figure 3.1* Trends in world energy use since 1860

The price of oil, on a downward trend throughout the 1950s and 1960s, rose from 1970 and then leapt in the famous 'oil crises' of 1973 and 1979, both powered by political conflicts in the Middle East – the second Arab–Israeli war in one case and the Iranian Revolution in the other. Thus, if one examines primary energy production and commercial energy consumption in the later 1970s and early 1980s, the picture is one of levelling off. Accelerating rates of energy use are no longer viewed as an automatic surrogate of economic development. And the secular nature of this transformation is demonstrably illustrated in the way the progressive collapse of the world oil market since 1981–2 has not prompted a new round of energy-intensive economic activity.

(Saudi-Arabian light crude in 1974 US dollars)

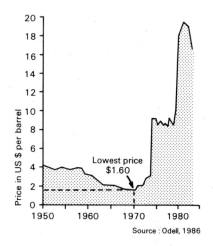

Source : Odell, 1986

Figure 3.2 The price of oil, 1950–83

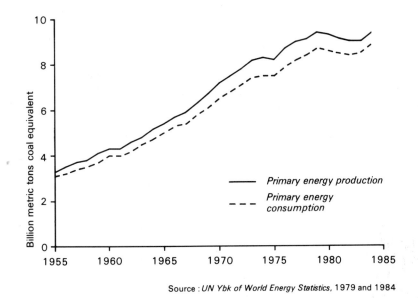

Source : *UN Ybk of World Energy Statistics*, 1979 and 1984

Figure 3.3 Energy production and consumption in the world, 1955–84

The rise of OPEC

The story of world energy production and consumption in the post-war decades is fundamentally the story of the rise of oil. Around 1950, oil's share in world energy *production* was slightly less than one-third. By 1973 it had risen to slightly over one-half. Even in the mid-1980s, in the wake of chronic instabilities in the international oil world, the proportion remained around 45 per cent. And this has been against the background of the growth of alternative energy sources like gas and electricity (hydro- and nuclear-generated). When the pattern of energy *consumption* is examined, the outcome is much the same (see Figure 3.4). The growing significance of oil has been accompanied by important developments in the industry's production organization, particularly in its political dimensions. Because so much oil is not consumed in the countries where it is produced, international trade in oil has become an intrinsic feature of the industry. In the USA, the world's first major oil producer, the internationalization of the oil market in the immediate post-war decades prompted the imposition of import quotas to protect the well-being of domestic production. Concurrently, growing major producers in areas like the Middle East, when faced with market protectionism and with a steady rise in the number of oil-producing states, sought political–economic combination. Thus was formed the Organization of Petroleum-Exporting Countries (OPEC), which aimed to obtain greater financial stability and improved profits both for producer nations and for international oil companies.

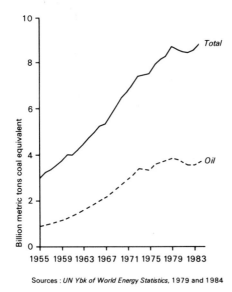

Sources : *UN Ybk of World Energy Statistics,* 1979 and 1984

Figure 3.4 World primary energy consumption, 1955–84: the share of oil

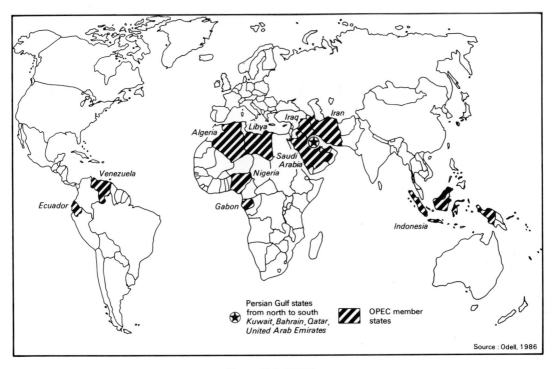

Figure 3.5 OPEC states

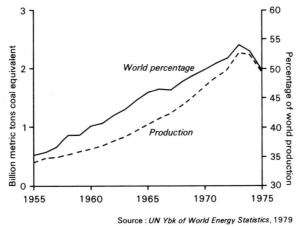

Source : *UN Ybk of World Energy Statistics*, 1979

Figure 3.6 OPEC oil production, 1955–75

The eclipse of OPEC power

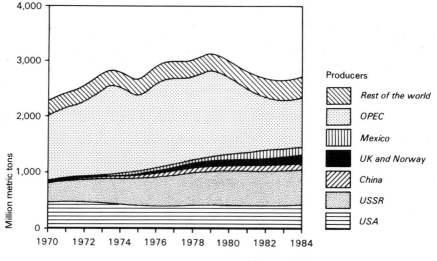

Source: *UN Ybk of World Energy Statistics*, 1984

Figure 3.7 Production of crude oil, 1970–84

For two decades from its foundation in 1960, OPEC dominated the world oil market, as Figure 3.7 demonstrates. By 1973 OPEC oil accounted for 36.5 per cent of all energy used in the non-communist world (excluding the OPEC states themselves). In the 1980s, however, OPEC's position declined. Production levels have fallen, in contrast to the expansion of North Sea and Mexican production. In 1983 OPEC oil accounted for only 19.5 per cent of all energy used in the non-communist world. EEC oil imports from OPEC, when measured against an index level of 100 in 1980, had dropped to 49 by 1985. The eclipse of OPEC power is not simply explained. The immediate cause, though, has been the weakening in oil prices since 1981–2 and their collapse in 1986. In 1986, spot-market prices for oil dipped below 10 US dollars per barrel, against a high of more than 30 in 1981. In each year from 1980 to 1986, OPEC recorded losses of oil sales. The stability of economic cartels is invariably affected in times of price weakness. However, OPEC's difficulties have been exacerbated by new additions to the world's oil-producing states. In 1972, for instance, the UK's contribution to world oil production was negligible. By 1983 it was 4.2 per cent. Over the same time-span, Venezuela (OPEC) saw its share fall from 6.5 to 3.5 per cent, Libya (OPEC) from 4.1 to 1.9 per cent, and Iran (OPEC) from

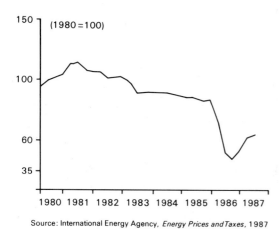

Source: International Energy Agency, *Energy Prices and Taxes*, 1987

Figure 3.8 Indices of crude oil import prices, 1980–7 (US dollars)

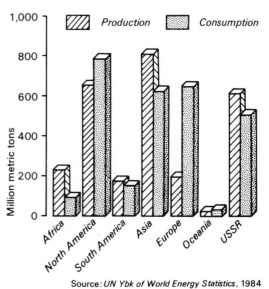

Figure 3.9 Production and consumption of crude petroleum, 1984

Source: *UN Ybk of World Energy Statistics*, 1984

9.6 to 4.6 per cent. All of these latter figures represent falls in production rather than just reduced shares of a larger overall output. Among the non-OPEC oil states, of which the UK is obviously one, Mexico has perhaps produced the most striking performance, accounting for 5.2 per cent of world production by 1983 against a base-point of less than 1 per cent in 1972. Non-OPEC producers have not in any way been insulated from falling oil prices, but for those that are relative newcomers to oil production the effects have understandably been less serious: these pro-ducers were never major beneficiaries of the price surges of 1973 and 1979. The USSR, the world's largest oil producer if OPEC is discounted, has certainly suffered rather more from declining oil prices, since some 50 per cent or more of its foreign exchange is derived from oil exports. However, Soviet oil production is now facing increasing problems of accessibility and there is already a transfer of emphasis towards gas production and nuclear power. Even so, between 1972 and 1983, the USSR increased its share of world oil production from 15.2 to 22.4 per cent.

The international oil trade

The five importing countries depicted in Figure 3.10 accounted for roughly half of all world imports of crude petroleum in 1984. Japan and the USA alone accounted for roughly one-third.

As the world's leading economic power, it comes as no surprise to find the USA among the principal oil importers. In 1938 the USA produced some 60 per cent of total world oil output and was a net exporter of oil. By 1983, however, it was producing only about 17 per cent of total world output and had been a growing net importer for some 35 years. In 1984, US production of crude petroleum failed to match demand by the order of 172 million metric tons, although before the 1979 oil crisis this dependency level had been even higher. In 1984, Mexico was the most important source of US imports (19.8 per cent), followed by the UK (10.5 per cent), Saudi Arabia (9.6 per cent), and Indonesia (9 per cent). After 1979, the USA made determined efforts to reduce its dependency on oil imports from the Middle East and from Africa. This was facilitated by a contraction in demand and the simultaneous growth of alternative suppliers like the UK. Between 1980 and 1983, US imports from the Middle East in fact fell by 73 per cent.

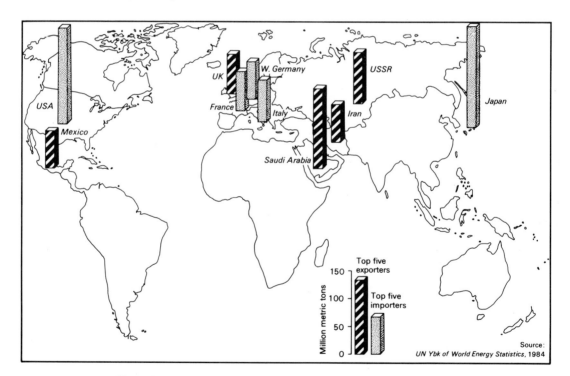

Figure 3.10 Principal importers/exporters of crude petroleum, 1984

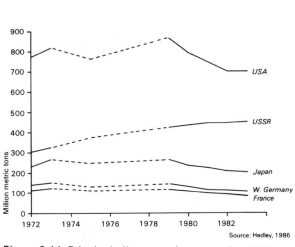

Figure 3.11 Principal oil-consuming countries, 1972–83

In 1984, Japan actually imported more crude petroleum than the USA (some 182 million metric tons). That such a small island nation is able to sustain so high a level of energy imports is testament to the enormous strength of the Japanese economic–industrial system. Moreover, this is a position which has been achieved over the course of three decades at most, for in 1957 Japanese oil consumption was less than 15 million metric tons. Unlike the USA, Japan remains heavily reliant upon the Middle East for its oil imports. In 1984, the primary sources were Saudi Arabia (32 per cent), the United Arab Emirates (15 per cent), Indonesia (12.7 per cent) and Iran (7 per cent). In common with the USA, Japanese oil consumption has fallen since 1979, notably in association with the decline of energy-intensive industries.

The remaining primary importers of crude petroleum in 1984 were all found in western Europe. Indeed, if one extends the list covered by the map to the top ten importers, western European states account for five. As in the case of Japan, imports on a scale of this sort reflect highly vigorous industrialized economies, participating in world markets. Italy, as the leading importer of the five, drew substantial supplies from Iran and Saudi Arabia, but Libya formed its primary single import source (15 per cent). France's principal sources were the UK and Nigeria (18.7 and 14.2 per cent); West Germany's likewise (26.6 and 14.2 per cent).

It is clear that there is a measure of symmetry between the principal petroleum importers and the principal petroleum exporters as depicted on the map. The fundamental exception, though, is the USSR. France, Italy, and West Germany all import oil from the USSR, but the aggregate in 1984 was only 20 per cent of the total Soviet export volume. The bulk (65 per cent) was distributed among the various centrally planned economies of eastern Europe, although this should not overlook the vital importance of 'western' oil exports as a source of hard currency. The USSR is also exceptional if one examines the principal oil-consuming countries. Figure 3.11 shows the countries of the world which consumed, on average, at least 100 million metric tons per annum between 1972 and 1983. Four out of five are principal importers, but the USSR, second in rank order of consumption, is a principal exporter. It comes as no surprise, therefore, to find that the USSR is the world's largest oil producer. The UK increasingly echoes this pattern of production for large-scale consumption *and* for export.

Coal

Coal was the foundation stone of the European industrial revolution and remained the primary energy source in the world until well into the twentieth century. Indeed, not until the mid-1960s did oil eclipse coal as the primary fuel of energy consumption; and in the 1980s, with the fall-off in world oil consumption, coal has begun to resume some of its former significance. Coal has been most successfully ousted by oil in the realms of industrial and domestic heating, and in transport. It remains vital in the metallurgical industries and retains a strong hold in electricity generation. In some countries, coal still dominates the energy sector. China affords the primary example. It consumes roughly five times as much coal as oil and over the 1970s grew to become the world's leading coal user, ahead of the USA and USSR.

Coal is not traded on the international commodity market in anything like the way that oil has come to be over the post-war decades. Primarily, this is because most coal is consumed in the countries where it is produced. The major coal reserves of the world are found in the USA, the USSR, and China. If so many major countries of the developed world have access to large coal supplies, one may well ask why oil is imported on such a scale. The answers are to be found in the relative cheapness of oil, particularly up to the mid-1970s, and the corresponding 'expensiveness' of coal, especially when it cannot be mined by surface methods. Coal is also an expensive commodity to transport, although the advent of bulk sea carriers has stimulated oceanic trade in coal, notably from Australia, South Africa, and the USA to places like Japan and western Europe.

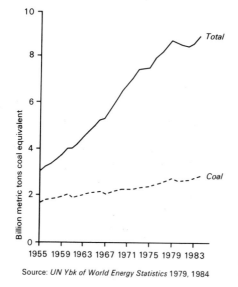

Source: *UN Ybk of World Energy Statistics* 1979, 1984

Figure 3.12 World primary energy consumption, 1955–84: the share of coal

56

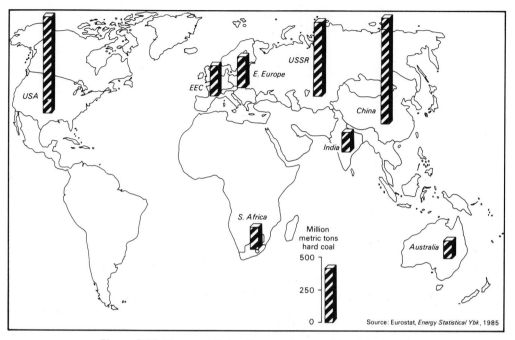

Figure 3.13 The world's leading producers of hard coal, 1985

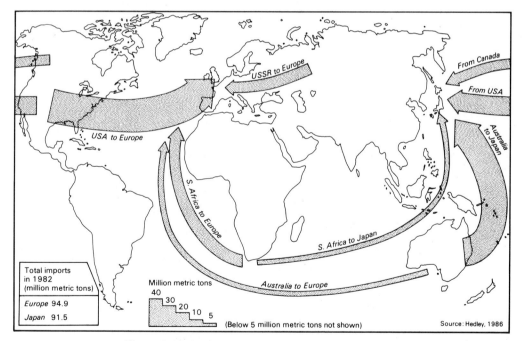

Figure 3.14 Principal oceanic coal movements, 1982

Natural gas

The use of gas as an energy source dates back to the industrial revolution in Europe. It was produced from coal and became generally known as 'town gas' by virtue of the necessity to make it in the localities where it was to be consumed. In England, the gasometer became a highly familiar part of the townscape, as well as an eyesore. Today, however, gas produced from coal has been largely superseded by natural gas from the substrata. Indeed, some geologists now consider that exploitable reserves of natural gas are as large as those of oil. In 1984 natural gas accounted for 19.5 per cent of the world's commercial energy consumption, as against 30 per cent for coal and 39.5 per cent for oil (all measured in million metric tons of oil equivalent). Thirty years earlier, before major gas fields like those in the Netherlands and Algeria were discovered and exploited, gas (town and natural) accounted for rather less than 12 per cent. The real gain, of course, is considerably greater than these figures imply, for a substantial part of natural gas production has been a direct replacement for town gas, especially in Europe.

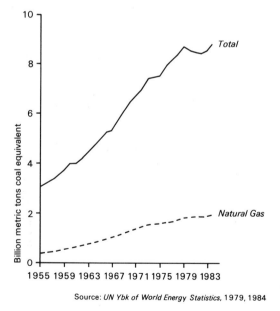

Source: *UN Ybk of World Energy Statistics*, 1979, 1984

Figure 3.15 World primary energy consumption, 1955–84: the share of natural gas

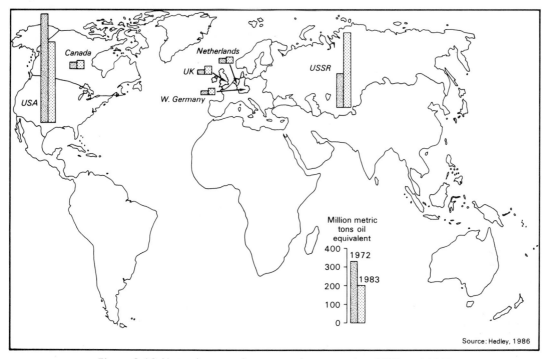

Figure 3.16 Natural gas: major consuming countries, 1972 and 1983

Natural gas frequently occurs in association with oil and has often been burnt off as waste. This still happens in countries where there is little or no demand for its use; but in the USA, Europe, the USSR, and other developed parts of the world, gas occurring in combination with oil is utilized extensively. Oil-associated gas clearly sets an autonomous control on natural-gas production and this is made the more difficult because gas is not easily transported or stored. Where natural gas occurs independently from oil, production is much more readily controlled. Some three-quarters of proven world gas reserves in 1985 were of this type, the USSR accounting for more than a third of them.

Like coal, gas is not an internationally traded commodity in the way that oil has become. Partly this is because most major producers are also major consumers. It is also due to the problems of transporting gas. The gas may be liquefied and then conveyed in bulk carriers, but this adds measurably to costs. The much more common method has been to transport by pipeline. Italy, for instance, has recently been receiving Algerian gas by pipeline under the Mediterranean, while the USSR has become a major exporter of gas to eastern and western Europe, by overland pipeline from Siberia. Even so, in 1982 only about 12 per cent of the world gas production was for export.

A map of producers for 1983 would not show a very different pattern from the one in Figure 3.16. The USA produced slightly less than it consumed (94 per cent), the USSR rather more (119 per cent). The USA and the USSR together accounted for two-thirds of world production in 1983. US gas consumption fell substantially in the early 1980s as a result of a complex of factors, including the reduced price of oil and deregulation of gas pricing which resulted in a general rise in prices.

Alternative energy sources

Nuclear power

On first sight nuclear power would appear to offer a solution to most of the world's energy problems. Potential uranium reserves are vast; indeed, uranium is a much more widely occurring resource than oil, coal, or natural gas. Nuclear power plants may be erected more or less anywhere: there is no requirement for consumption to be at or near the site of production given the very small quantities of uranium fuel necessary. This is a formidable advantage alongside the expense of coal carriage or the way the major oil-producing countries are not the major consumers of oil, necessitating a massive international oil trade. However, nuclear energy is highly expensive in terms of installation, research, and development. Since the rise of environmentalism, moreover, it has become a highly sensitive public-policy issue in the major western democracies. Superficially, nuclear power may be 'clean'. But all plants produce highly dangerous wastes which require disposal; and the potential dangers from a major reactor accident are vast, as was so clearly demonstrated in the Chernobyl disaster in the Russian Ukraine in April 1986.

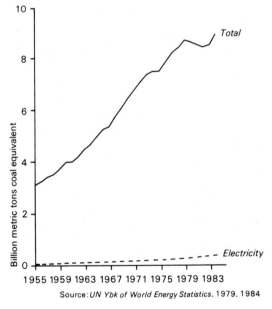

Source: *UN Ybk of World Energy Statistics*, 1979, 1984

Figure 3.17 World primary energy consumption, 1955–84: the share of hydro, nuclear, and geothermal sources

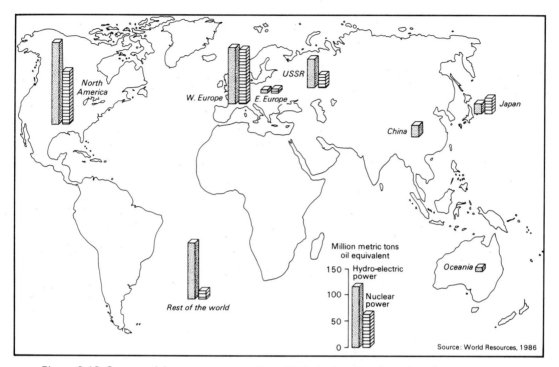

Figure 3.18 Commercial energy consumption, 1984: hydro-electric and nuclear components

These factors have meant that the major focus of nuclear energy development has been in countries with very limited indigenous supplies of conventional fuels, in countries with well-developed scientific and technical skills and the capital to apply them, and in countries with strong, centrally organized administrative regimes, often but not always socialist in orientation. Thus does one find that France has the highest proportion of its electricity generated by nuclear power, planned to rise to 70 per cent by the year 1990. In the USSR, meanwhile, an ambitious nuclear programme has been instituted which saw capacity expanding at 35 per cent per annum over the 1970s to make some 10 per cent of electricity generated by nuclear means by 1981. A similar pace of expansion had been planned up to the millennium, although the Chernobyl accident may retard realization of such a goal.

Hydro-electric power

In recent decades nuclear power has been the most rapidly growing sector of world commercial energy consumption, but in 1984 it remained well behind hydro-electric power in simple percentage terms (supplying 3.9 per cent against 6.7 per cent of the world total). Some countries, Canada principal among them, rely very heavily on HEP for electricity generation (accounting for approximately 50 per cent). In developing countries, the HEP contribution to total commercial energy consumption is roughy eight times that of nuclear power and there remains great potential for further HEP development, especially in the states of South America. HEP suffers from none of the environmental hazards of the nuclear industry, but in the developed world, particularly in Europe, the development potential has largely been utilized.

Rich world, poor world

The socio-economic division of the world into rich nations and poor, into developed, developing, and underdeveloped states, is a commonplace of which few will today be unaware. While some commentators have argued against so simplistic a differentiation, it is startlingly the case that in world energy consumption, nearly two-thirds is accounted for by the two super-powers, by Japan, and by the twelve states of the EEC. As Figure 3.20 shows, these nations together accounted for only 20 per cent of the world's entire population in 1984. The USA, with approximately 5 per cent of the world population, made up for one-quarter of world energy consumption in 1984. The same kinds of contrast emerge when one examines energy consumption per capita. By the 1970s, in the developed market economies of the world, levels were around 6,000 kg per capita, almost double the level of the 1950s. The centrally planned economies revealed a similar doubling, but at an altogether lower level of consumption: some 2,000 kg per capita by 1979. Meanwhile, in the developing market economies, consumption levels in 1979 were roughly one-sixteenth of those in the developed market economies. Even among OPEC states, with their windfall oil profits, the pattern is barely different.

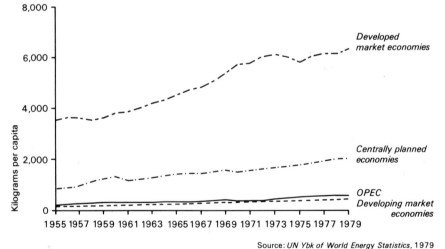

Source: *UN Ybk of World Energy Statistics*, 1979

Figure 3.19 Energy consumption per capita, 1955–79

The developing world's major problem over energy consumption in recent decades has been how to cope with dramatic price increases. This problem has naturally been most acute for net importers, particularly of oil. The developed world responded to the oil-price increases in a variety of ways, some forced, some by design. Improved efficiency of energy use was one area where the impact was capable of being absorbed without a major deleterious effect on production. Some scope also existed for energy substitution. However, in the developing world such escape routes were limited in their significance, if they were available at all. Capacities for energy-conservation measures, for instance, are barely consistent with developing economic systems. This is yet more clearly demonstrated when indigenous energy resources in the developing world are considered. Timber remains a fundamental supplier of energy in much of Africa and South Asia, but in many areas scarcity is growing. Given that rates of world population expansion are greatest in these continental regions, the problems will intensify unless there are deliberate measures to husband woodland resources. For some commentators, it is here that the world's real energy crisis is actually to be found.

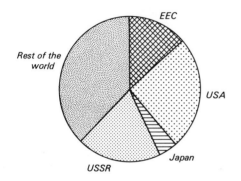

Figure 3.20a Share of world energy consumption, 1984

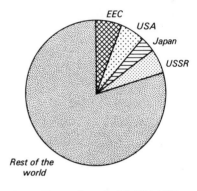

Source : Eurostat, *Energy Statistical Ybk*, 1985

Figure 3.20b Share of world population, 1984

Part of London dockland, once a mecca of manufacturing, but now largely de-industrialized

4

Industry

Manufacturing

Manufacturing exports

Industrial divisions

Iron

Steel

Motor-vehicle manufacture

The resource prospect

Manufacturing

Manufacturing forms one of the most fascinating dimensions of the world economy. It can be distinguished from the agriculture and energy sectors because of the way in which it is so much more divorced from the world of nature. This is not to say that it does not utilize the materials of nature. It is simply that manufacturing involves a scale and type of resource conversion which creates a production dimension all of its own. Under capitalism, moreover, this aspect has developed an acuteness that it might not otherwise have possessed. This is perhaps most vividly expressed in the high concentration of world manufacturing production (excluding the centrally planned economies) in western Europe and North America. And the apotheosis of the pattern is surely represented in Japan: a diminutive island state, bereft of major natural resources, and yet by 1985 able to account for roughly 15 per cent of world manufacturing output, exclusive of the CPEs.

As the first industrial nation, Britain led the world in manufacturing output for much of the nineteenth century, but by the twentieth it had been joined by the USA and various other European states; and, with the exception of Japan, the position has changed little since the Second World War. In 1970, six western countries together with Japan accounted for three-quarters of world manufacturing output, excluding the CPEs. In 1985, the same countries accounted for just above two-thirds, the principal changes being that Japan's contribution had grown by 50 per cent, whereas most of the major western states, headed by the USA, had contracted. And perhaps signifying the shape of things to come, Brazil was vying with Canada in rank, followed by Spain and Mexico.

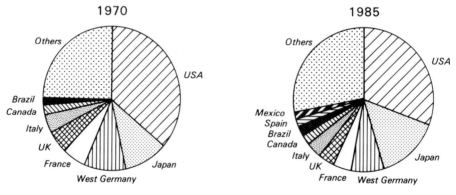

Source : World Bank, *World Development Report*, 1988

Figure 4.1 Share of world manufacturing output (excluding centrally planned economies), 1970 and 1985

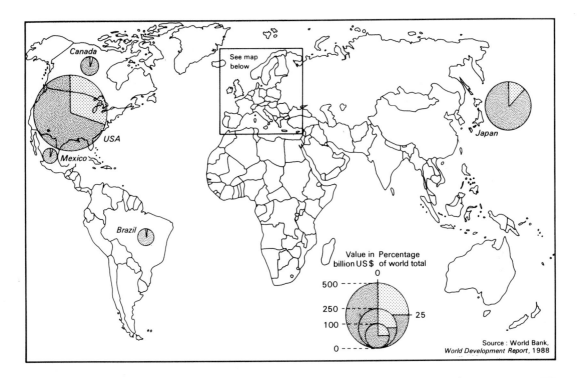

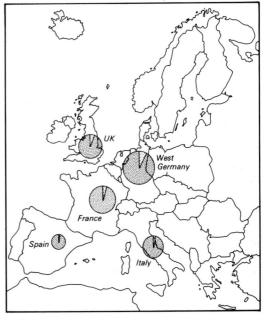

Figure 4.2 Top ten manufacturing nations in 1985, by manufacturing value added in current US dollars (excluding centrally planned economies)

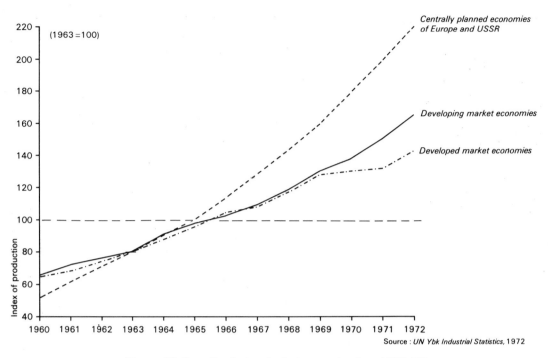

Figure 4.3 Growth of manufacturing production, 1960–72

It is not possible to examine manufacturing output from the socialist world in terms which yield a valid comparison with the figures and diagrams presented on the preceding pages. Even were it possible to do so, the usefulness of such an exercise would be limited given the fundamentally different form of the social relations of production in most centrally planned systems. The pattern of geographical concentration and change that these pages depict is a function primarily of capitalist development. As such, the CPEs are of marginal relevance, even if their manufactured goods have increasingly featured in international trade since about 1970.

Leaving aside the absolute dimensions of world manufacturing output, it can be seen from Figures 4.3 and 4.4 that the developed market economies of the west have shown a lesser rate of expansion than either the developing market economies, or even the USSR

and its eastern European satellites. In the years 1960 to 1972, in particular, the centrally planned economies revealed a vigorous acceleration relative to the world's market economies. And, whereas in the period 1972 to 1984, the developed market economies were registering the impact of the oil-price shocks and related recessionary trends, the centrally planned economies were able to maintain growth. Even the developing market economies showed a greater resilience in the face of recession. Naturally, these trends must be viewed in the light of the relative scales of the manufacturing sectors in the three economic groupings: the recession of the 1970s and 1980s, for example, could not fail to have a greater impact in the developed market economies than in the developing – simply by virtue of a vastly greater manufacturing capacity. In the case of the centrally planned economies, moreover, one has to bear in mind the greater significance of the manufacturing sector in the broad band of economic activity.

Within the developing capitalist world in recent years, a major catalyst has been represented by small groups of minor states in Southeast Asia: Hong Kong, Singapore, Taiwan, and South Korea. In 1963, the four accounted for approximately 0.35 per cent of world manufacturing output (excluding the CPEs); by 1980 it was around 1.55 per cent, that is only 60 per cent less than the UK share. In Latin America, Brazil and Mexico together accounted for some 5 per cent of world output (excluding CPEs) by 1980, readily vying with leading states of western Europe. Whereas over the 1970s western industrial nations recorded about a 30 per cent growth in manufacturing output, South Korea achieved a fivefold rate, while Brazil's rate doubled.

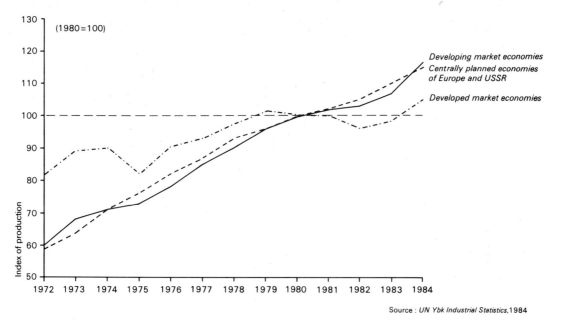

Source : *UN Ybk Industrial Statistics*, 1984

Figure 4.4 Growth of manufacturing production, 1972–84

Manufacturing exports

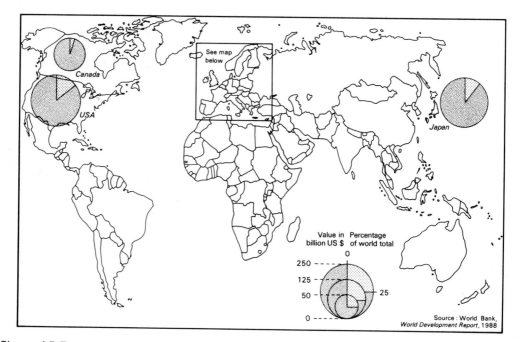

Figure 4.5 Top ten manufacturing exporters in 1986, by value of manufacturing exports in US dollars (excluding centrally planned economies)

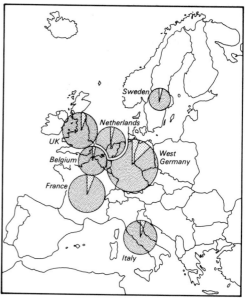

The enormous concentration of the free world's manufacturing output in the various 'core' states of the west cannot, of course, be understood simply in terms of domestic demand. In 1985, for instance, West Germany's manufacturing output (measured in value added in current US dollars) was as much as a quarter of that of the USA, a performance that can be understood only in the context of the size of the export base of West German manufacture. In 1986, in fact, the country led the free world in terms of its contribution to world manufacturing exports. At 12.7 per cent of the total, it eclipsed the USA on only 11.4 per cent. In a rather similar way, Belgium, with 3.6 per cent of world manufacturing exports in 1986 and ranking ninth, accounted for only 0.7 per cent of the free world's manufacturing output in 1985, ranking but fifteenth.

It was Britain in the later nineteenth century that pioneered the export-base economy, aided by the trading monopolies which came from empire. In recent times, the UK's manufacturing exports have become a shadow of their former state, in the early 1980s falling to below 5 per cent of the free-world total, eclipsed first by West Germany and, increasingly, by other European states. Moreover, the scale of West Germany's performance has been matched in the Far East, in Japan. By 1986, Japan was accounting for some 11 per cent of the free world's manufacturing exports, a position accomplished over little more than a quarter of a century. Of much less absolute impact but impressive in the relative scale of its growth has been the record of some of the minor states of Southeast Asia. By 1986, for instance, South Korea accounted for 1.3 per cent of world manufacturing exports.

If the output value of the top ten manufacturing exporters is examined on a per-capita basis, the dominance of the western European states is considerably enhanced. In these terms, the USA takes on a significantly lower status, as indeed does Japan. The records set by the Low Countries are clearly in part a reflection of a manufacturing capacity which is geared to higher-value goods.

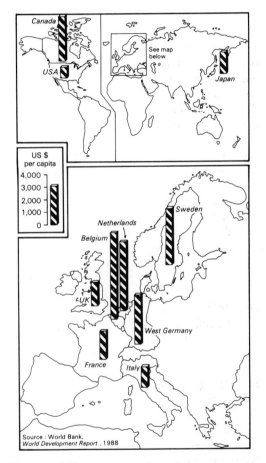

Figure 4.6 Top ten manufacturing exporters in 1986, related to population bases

Industrial divisions

It is easy to think of manufacturing and industry as synonymous terms. And in the developed market economies of the west, as well as in the developed socialist block, one would not be altogether amiss. As Figure 4.7 illustrates, manufacturing accounted for 83.2 per cent and 88.2 per cent, respectively, in these major production realms in 1980, according to UN sources. If one examines the category of developing market economies, however, the pattern is not sustained. Here one finds that manufacturing is almost on a level with mining and quarrying. As the latter includes the extraction of crude petroleum and natural gas, the result is hardly surprising. If one pursues a different path of disaggregation and examines the geographical category comprising the countries of the Asian Middle East, of East Asia and Southeast Asia, but excluding Israel and Japan, the percentage for mining and quarrying rises to 61.1 and manufacturing falls to 35.9. Inclusive of Japan and Israel, the figures become 30.2 and 63.9 respectively, providing a further vivid demonstration of the force of Japanese manufacturing capacity.

These various sectoral differences have been important in regulating the effects of economic crises within the capitalist world. The dramatic fall in the index of production for mining and quarrying in the developing market economies is a particular case in point. Sectors of primary production are typically more seriously affected than secondary (manufacturing) ones, although the pattern depicted here must in part reflect the increasing significance of indigenous oil and gas deposits in areas such as north-west Europe, contributing to a more secular downward trend in demand elsewhere. Once again, if one focuses on the geographical grouping comprising countries of the Asian Middle East, of East Asia and Southeast Asia, but excluding Japan and Israel, the fall in the index for mining and quarrying stands out even more sharply. Between 1977 and 1984, it dropped from 125 to 66.

By the nature of their political–economic systems, the centrally planned economies of the USSR and eastern Europe record little of the fluctuation found in the capitalist world, although it is certain that in actuality there is rather less evenness than the graph predicts. Perhaps the most significant features of the CPEs is the very great dominance of the manufacturing sector, and, by the same token, a utilities sector half the size of that in the developed west. Both features might be seen to reflect the lesser position of the CPEs on the Rostovian development schema.

Developed market economies = North America, Europe (ex. CPEs and Yugoslavia), Australia, Israel, Japan, New Zealand, and South Africa.
 Developing market economies = Caribbean, Central and South America, Africa (ex. South Africa), Asian Middle East and East and Southeast Asia (other than Israel and Japan), and Yugoslavia.
 Centrally planned economies = Bulgaria, Czechoslovakia, GDR, Hungary, Poland, Romania, and the USSR.

Industry

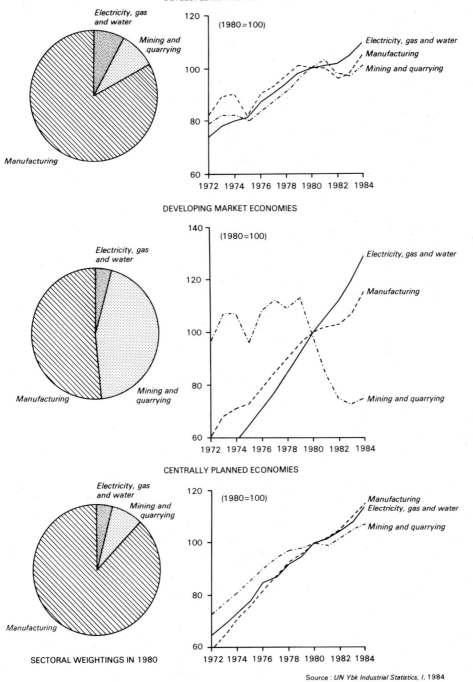

DEVELOPED MARKET ECONOMIES

Electricity, gas and water
Mining and quarrying
Manufacturing

(1980=100)
Electricity, gas and water
Manufacturing
Mining and quarrying

DEVELOPING MARKET ECONOMIES

Electricity, gas and water
Mining and quarrying
Manufacturing

(1980=100)
Electricity, gas and water
Manufacturing
Mining and quarrying

CENTRALLY PLANNED ECONOMIES

Electricity, gas and water
Mining and quarrying
Manufacturing

(1980=100)
Manufacturing
Electricity, gas and water
Mining and quarrying

SECTORAL WEIGHTINGS IN 1980

Source : *UN Ybk Industrial Statistics, I,* 1984

Figure 4.7 Industrial production, 1972–84

Iron

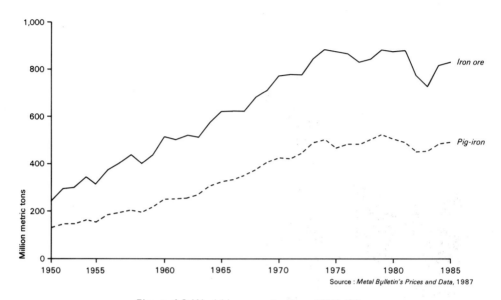

Source : *Metal Bulletin's Prices and Data*, 1987

Figure 4.8 World iron production, 1950–85

Iron and steel represent two of the most basic elements of industrial civilization. At times, consumption levels have grown more rapidly than gross domestic product. And for some economic commentators, the development of a country's iron and steel industry has been viewed as both ingredient and agent of industrial 'take-off'.

World iron-ore production showed a fairly consistent upward trend from 1950 until the economic depression of the mid-1970s. Since then the tendency has been contraction but with a much greater scale of fluctuation. However, the fall-off in demand is not simply a function of depressed economic conditions. Improved technology of manufacture and substitution of alternative metals have also exercised an impact.

Iron is a relatively widely occurring metal, but it is found in commercially recoverable quantities in relatively few parts of the world. The nineteenth-century iron and steel industries grew upon rich, locally available deposits and ushered in an age of relatively cheap mass production which quickly established for iron and steel an almost universal usage in the industrialized world. The subsequent history of the industry, therefore, has been one geared to low-cost, mass production. As regards iron-ore deposits, this has entailed a world-wide search for high-grade ores or ores that may be worked cheaply and in bulk. Thus the USA, formerly well supplied with ores from the vast Lake Superior deposits, imported some 10 million tonnes from Canada in 1983. Some 5.3 million tonnes of Canadian ore also found its way to Britain. The USSR is now the world's largest ore producer with its enormous

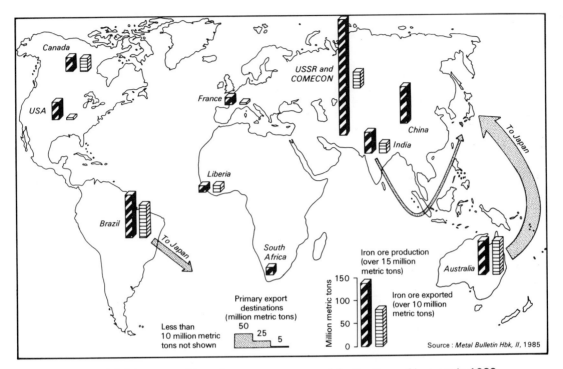

Figure 4.9 Primary world producers, exporters, and destinations of iron ore in 1983

deposits in the Ural Mountains. Other major world producers are Brazil, Australia, India, and Liberia. Australia and Brazil each export very high proportions of their ore to Japan. A lesser volume is similarly exported from India.

The world production of pig-iron since 1950 has generally followed the pattern of iron-ore production, although with a lesser margin of fluctuation, notably in the period since the first oil crisis. The USSR accounted for nearly a quarter of total world production in 1983, while the continent of Europe accounted for slightly more than a quarter. Japan, despite its dearth of ore reserves and the need to import coking coal from Canada and Australia, made up 15 per cent of world production in 1983. Of the remainder, the USA contributed some 9 per cent and China 8.8 per cent.

The overwhelming dominance of the developed industrial states in world pig-iron manufacture is a startling reminder of the stability and inertia of the world economic order, notwithstanding the increasing reliance upon vast iron-ore supplies from states of the developing world. Brazil, despite its large ore output, accounted for only 2.6 per cent of world pig-iron capacity in 1983. The entire continent of Africa contributed only 1.7 per cent. Perhaps even more surprising, though, is the situation of Australia. Despite major ore deposits and an advanced economy, its pig-iron capacity is minor: around 1 per cent of world production in 1983. In 1983, Australia actually exported more ore than it mined (some of it obviously from accumulated stocks). Two-thirds of this was shipped to Japan, where the economy of manufacture is such that Japanese products can undercut the delivery prices of some US producers selling in their own backyard.

Steel

The trend of world raw-steel production from 1950 to the mid-1980s follows much the same pattern as that for pig-iron, although absolute magnitudes are greater in steel than in iron on account of the significance of scrap as a direct input in raw-steel production. The geography of raw-steel production in the mid-1980s bears predictable similarity to the pattern of pig-iron manufacture. The USSR boasted the largest single national output in 1984, representing a little over one-fifth of the world total, followed by the EEC (16.7 per cent) and Japan 14.8 per cent). The USA, once a world leader in steel production, has seen its position slip progressively since the 1960s. Some leading steel producers in Europe, the UK and West Germany among them, have followed a similar path of contraction. The explanation for these locational shifts in the primary centres of gravity of production is not easily established. Advances in maritime transport technology have certainly been critical in allowing resource-deficit nations like Japan to become major producers, confounding most of the locational traditions and conventions established in the nineteenth and early twentieth centuries. Nevertheless, in less than a quarter-century, Japan has undoubtedly created the most efficient steel industry in the world, such that by around 1980 it was able to account for a third of all world steel exports. Other factors in the declining significance of the traditional western producers relate largely to evolving economic structures. Whereas in the developing world, especially in the newly industrializing countries, steel demands have been intensifying, in post-industrial systems they have been declining as the thrust of manufacturing shifts from basic sectors like ship-building and engineering to the realms of higher technology and as the tertiary and quaternary sectors expand at the expense of primary and secondary economic activities.

As Figure 4.12 demonstrates, raw-steel production is very much the domain of 'big business', and in some cases is in direct state ownership or control. The vast costs of running a competitive, modern steel industry help to explain both of these characteristics, although state involvement occurs for reasons of both military and economic strategy.

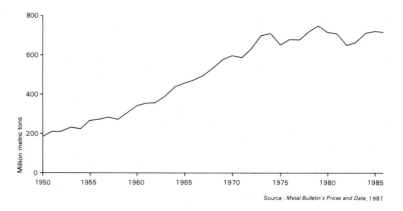

Source : *Metal Bulletin's Prices and Data*, 1987

Figure 4.10 World raw-steel production, 1950–86

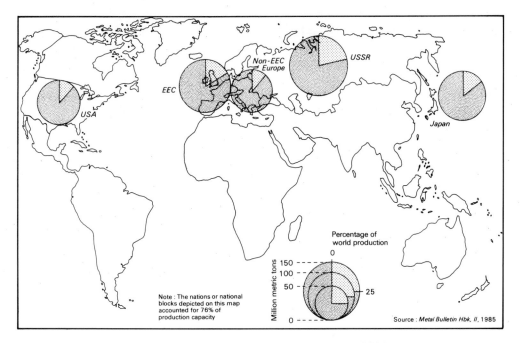

Figure 4.11 World raw-steel production in 1984

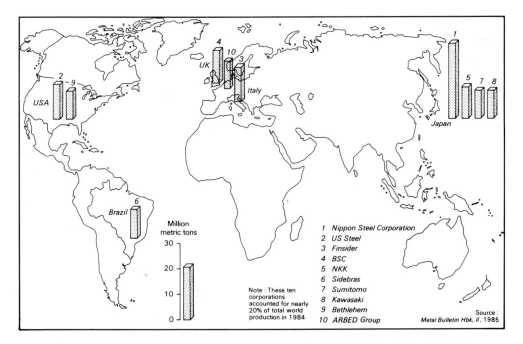

Figure 4.12 Top ten raw-steel making corporations in 1984 (excluding USSR)

Motor-vehicle manufacture

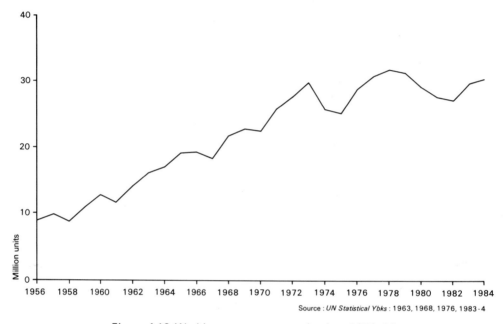

Source : *UN Statistical Ybks* : 1963, 1968, 1976, 1983-4

Figure 4.13 World passenger-car production, 1956–84

Of all the world's manufacturing sectors in the post-war era, motor vehicles must represent one of the most vital. In some leading western nations, it emerged as the premier growth sector of manufacturing over the 1950s and 1960s; and, in lesser developed nations, productive capacity in motor vehicles came to be viewed as an essential ingredient in strategies for economic growth. In some advanced states of the western world by 1980, motor-vehicle production was directly employing roughly one manufacturing worker in ten. By the early 1980s, some 15 per cent of world trade in manufactures was represented by motor vehicles.

Around 1960, the economies of western Europe and the USA accounted for the lion's share of world car output. Some two decades later, Japan had established itself as the world's leading car producer; output had expanded throughout mainland western Europe; South America had become established as a growing focus of production; but output in the UK and the USA had declined. However, owing to the increasingly transnational character of production and organization, these observed manufacturing shifts are not as significant as they may initially appear. By 1982, for instance, the US-based Ford Motor Company had some 60 per cent

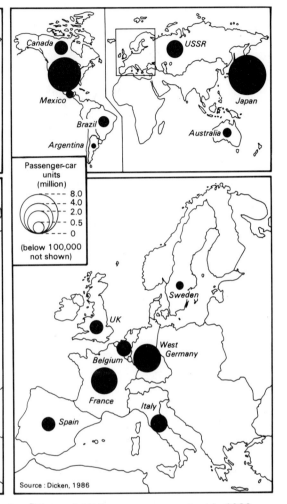

Figure 4.14 Passenger-car output in 1960

Figure 4.15 Passenger-car output in 1982

of its production capacity located outside the USA. In other words, it is increasingly less relevant to examine motor-vehicle production within the framework of the nation-state. This applies yet more forcefully where major companies have engaged in collaborative development projects. Naturally, the nation-state remains significant in employment terms and in accumulated capital, but in production its partitioning role has faded; even socialist eastern Europe has not been immune to penetration.

The singular advantage of the motor-vehicle sector in the 1950s and 1960s was that it was tapping a largely novel market. The industry's task was thus one of providing a product to a population which had little prior experience of it. By the 1970s, however, the pattern had altered. The oil-price shocks of 1973–4 and 1979–80 depressed the pace of growth through their effects on the economics of both production and consumption. A more secular difficulty flowed from the problem of approaching market saturation in the western

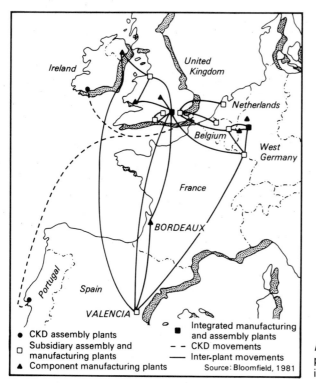

Figure 4.16 The organization of production of Ford vehicles in Europe in 1978

Legend:
- ● CKD assembly plants
- ☐ Subsidiary assembly and manufacturing plants
- ▲ Component manufacturing plants
- ■ Integrated manufacturing and assembly plants
- - - CKD movements
- —— Inter-plant movements

Source: Bloomfield, 1981

developed economies. Motor-vehicle production had necessarily to become oriented more towards replacement demand, except in so far as new markets were emerging in lesser developed economies around the world. The outcome was that by the later 1970s and early 1980s, the motor-vehicle production sector was in a state of flux. Profits fell, production was curtailed, plants were closed, and some national governments were drawn to intervene with financial rescue packages of varying forms. At the same time, manufacturers sought to enhance their efficiency through new production and marketing strategies. Competition intensified, finding clearest geographical expression in the growth of international trade in passenger vehicles. Japan has proved the most successful in this field, accounting for some 20 per cent of the domestic markets of the USA and the Low

Countries by the early 1980s. With some 3.8 million cars sold overseas in 1982, it readily eclipsed its nearest rival, West Germany, with an export of only 2.2 million. In the search for production economies, companies have forged transnational systems of manufacturing, exploiting differentials in the costs, skills, and reliability of labour. Where the traditions of the motor industry have been towards agglomeration, reflecting its 'assembly' or horizontally integrated form, the past decade has seen a growing spatial separation in the manufacturing operation (see Figure 4.16).

The relative volatility of motor-vehicle production, as a consumer-goods sector, is readily apparent in Figure 4.17, a time-series of car output in selected national economies covering the years from 1950 to 1986. Indeed, what these graphs demonstrate is the merit of a vigorous export sector in alleviating the pro-

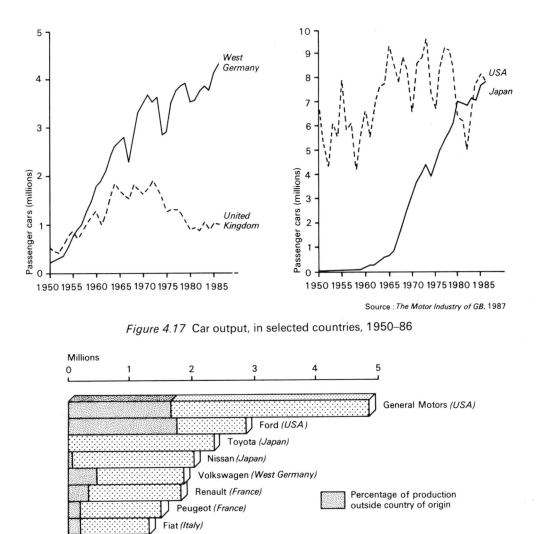

Source: *The Motor Industry of GB*, 1987

Figure 4.17 Car output, in selected countries, 1950–86

Source: Dicken, 1986

Figure 4.18 Passenger-car output by company, 1982

duction problems which derive from fluctuations in domestic consumption, from whatever origin. Thus does Japan sustain a much more even trend than the USA; and the West German pattern affords a not dissimilar parallel. Perhaps the most singular feature of the graphs, though, is the remarkable collapse of UK car production from the first oil crisis. In 1986, UK output was eclipsed in western Europe by West Germany (4.31 m.), France (2.77 m.), Italy (1.65 m.) and Spain (1.28 m.). The pattern reflects a massive growth in import penetration on the one hand, and the special problems of the UK motor-vehicle industry on the other. Among the latter one might single out persistent labour strife, low productivity, and poor quality.

The resource prospect

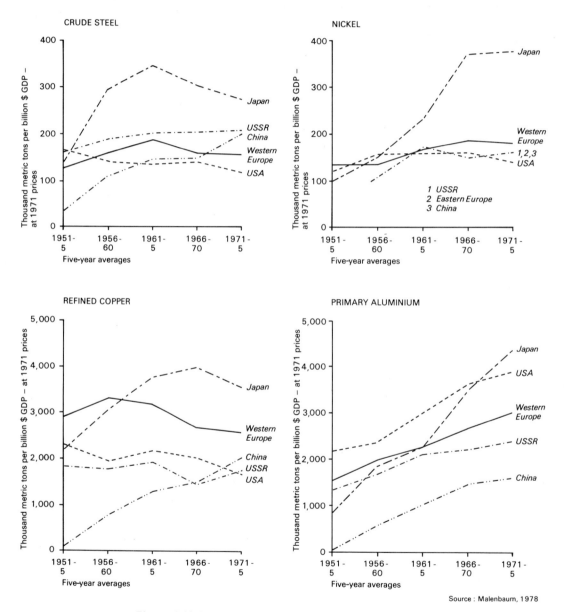

Figure 4.19 Intensity of use of selected metals, 1950–75

The accelerating trends of finite-resource use in the western world in the first post-war decades led many commentators to fear a major resource crisis, especially in non-ferrous metals, by the turn of the millennium. It was generally perceived that rising levels of economic growth (as measured in GDP per capita) were inextricably correlated with an increasing intensity of resource use, and that, short of major new resource discoveries, western man was destined for an era of economic deceleration and uncertainty, bringing in its wake increasing political instability. Subsequent research and subsequent events, however, have demonstrated that these fears have limited foundation. Figure 4.20, for example, presents an approximation of the relationship that has been observed between intensity of resource use and rising GDP per capita. As is clear, the curve is an inverted-U. Beyond certain levels of GDP per capita, intensity of use begins to decline. This occurs through technological developments which lead to greater efficiency in resource utilization; it occurs through the substitution of a more plentifully available metal for a less plentifully available one; it occurs because material requirements are becoming less significant inputs in the production of the goods and services that human society seeks.

These trends become apparent when one examines intensity-of-use patterns in some of the metals in common industrial use (see Figure 4.19). Steel and refined copper provide two primary examples where intensities have declined or stabilized among the major world users. Nickel echoes the pattern to a rather lesser degree. Only in primary aluminium is the experience one of continuing growth in intensity. This is explained largely by the widespread substitution of aluminium for

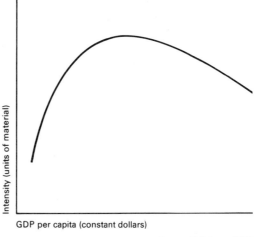

GDP per capita (constant dollars)

Source : Malenbaum, 1978

Figure 4.20 Intensity of resource use and GDP per capita

other metals like steel and copper, a trend which seems likely to intensify.

The formidable prominence of Japan in all four of the graphs underlines once again the strength and magnitude of Japanese post-war industrialization. Naturally this must be viewed in the context of an extensive export of finished industrial goods, considerably greater than either the USA or western Europe, though not, of course, minimizing the achievement in any way. Indeed, Japan's record is considerably enhanced when it is realized that military production is a significant metal-consumer in countries like the USA and the USSR. Aside from Japan, one cannot fail to note the record of China. If one needed evidence to support the proposition that the Chinese, since the communist revolution, had entered the realms of the developed world, it is surely here in these four graphs.

Empty container ship at the port of Southampton, powerful symbol of the United Kingdom's massive trade deficit

5

National income

Gross national product relative to population

Income distribution

Rates of growth in the developed world

Rates of growth in the developing world

The structure of production: agriculture

The structure of production: industry and services

Debt

Foreign aid

Gross national product relative to population

One of the most commonly used indicators of national income is GNP* per capita. Figure 5.1 charts national variations in GNP per capita in 1984 according to the calculations of the World Bank. Ethiopia recorded the lowest figure (110 US dollars per capita), the United Arab Emirates the highest (21,920 US dollars per capita). In general terms, the pattern of income depicted on the map holds few surprises. The strength of the capitalist core in the west is readily apparent, as is the industrial vigour of Japan. Major oil exporters like Saudi Arabia and Libya also feature prominently. It may come as a surprise to learn that Libya enjoyed roughly the same GNP per capita in 1984 as did the UK (8,500 US dollars), but that is the measure of the rewards provided by oil revenues in relatively unpopulated states in the desert regions. Perhaps the most revealing dimension of this data, though, is one which is not apparent from the map. It is that some 51 per cent of the world's population in 1984 lived in countries registering GNPs of less than 500 US dollars per capita. The contrast is with the industrial market economies which accounted for just 15 per cent of world population and enjoyed an average GNP per capita (weighted) of 11,430 US dollars. Switzerland headed that particular league in 1984, with a value of 16,330 US dollars.

The compilation of GNP statistics which may be directly compared, one nation against another, is an exceedingly difficult task and the data displayed on these pages must be viewed in this light. The need to translate national statistics into a common system of values is perhaps the most formidable of the problems. But the statistical bases themselves vary in nature and reliability; furthermore, data are not available for much of the socialist world. Another weakness stems from expressing the common values on the basis of heads of population. The implication is that entire national populations contribute equally to GNP and, in turn, derive equally in terms of income. The reality is otherwise, as the ensuing pages illustrate.

* The World Bank defines GNP as 'the total domestic and foreign output claimed by residents, calculated without making reductions for depreciation'.

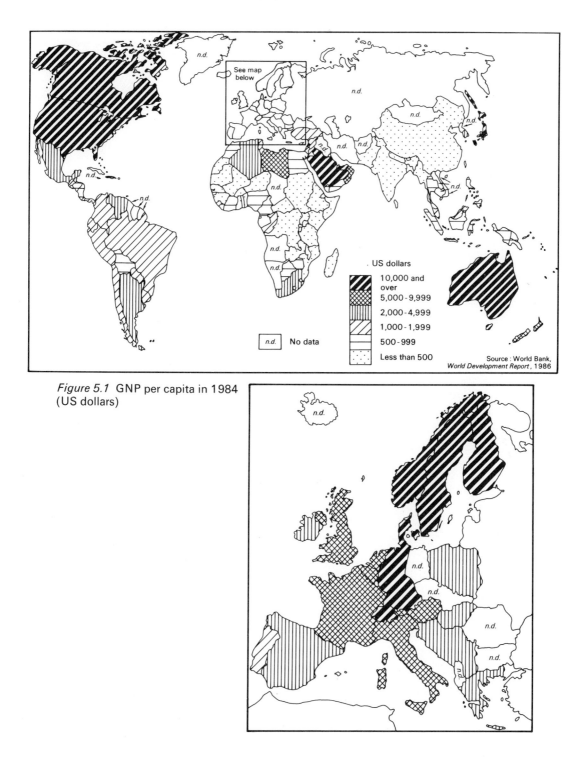

Figure 5.1 GNP per capita in 1984
(US dollars)

US dollars

10,000 and over

5,000 - 9,999

2,000 - 4,999

1,000 - 1,999

500 - 999

Less than 500

n.d. No data

Source : World Bank,
World Development Report, 1986

Income distribution

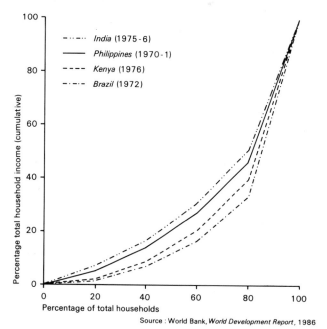

Source : World Bank, *World Development Report*, 1986

Figure 5.2 Estimated household-income distribution in four developing countries

For many Third World peoples, not only do they labour under exceptionally low levels of national product relative to the developed west, but what limited income is generated is often distributed in highly skewed fashion.

Once again, data on such a theme are very imperfect, especially outside the capitalist west. But the broad trends can be fairly readily sketched out. Among the low-income economies of Bangladesh, India, and Kenya in the

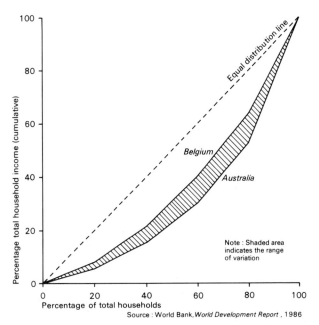

Source : World Bank, *World Development Report* , 1986

Figure 5.3 Household-income distribution in eighteen western economies (circa 1975–81)

mid-1970s, for example, some 52 per cent of household income accrued to the top 20 per cent of households. Conversely, the lowest 20 per cent of households received only 5 per cent of total household income. This compares with eighteen western industrial market economies, circa 1975–81, where the parallel figures were 40 per cent and 6.5 per cent respectively. Among eight lower-middle-income economies in the mid-1970s, the parallel figures were 53.5 and 4.7 per cent. Included in this group was Peru, which in 1972 had 61 per cent of income accruing to the top 20 per cent of households and only 1.9 per cent to the bottom 20 per cent. Another South American state, Brazil, generally classified as an upper-middle-income economy, recorded equivalent figures of 66.6 and 2.0 per cent in 1972. The apparent inference is that socio-economic development in the Third World has not generally been accompanied by much redistribution of income. However, this is to carry the data to the limits of explanation. And one has also to confront the fact that households vary in size, both *between* and

within nations. A more refined measure of income distribution would thus be one which distinguished per capita household income, but this is rarely available.

Figure 5.3 indicates the range of variation in household-income distribution for the principal industrial market economies of the west. Household size is less variable here than in the developing world; the data are also more reliably based. The most significant feature of the trend displayed is its limited variation. Beyond that, it is clear that income distribution is strongly skewed. The top 20 per cent of households accounted for between 36 and 47 per cent of total household income, with a mean of 40 and a standard deviation of 1.8; Australia, France, New Zealand, and Italy all recorded values above two standard deviations of the mean (47.1, 45.85, 44.7, and 43.9 per cent respectively). In the same four countries, 60 per cent of households accounted for less than a third of total household income. Perhaps the most significant contrast with states of the developing world is the presence of a more strongly defined middle class.

Rates of growth in the developed world

The rate of economic growth is one of the most singular preoccupations of the modern capitalist world. It has become one of the watchwords of government, in developing as well as developed states, while economic commentators, both academic and applied, are obsessed with it. Growth rates are scrutinized over long, medium, and short time-scales. There is a fascination with the 'ups' and 'downs' of growth and with its cyclical characteristics. There is a perennial search for 'origins', as if this might provide a golden key with which to unlock all the secrets of the capitalist dynamic. Among those who are familiar with the writings of Karl Marx, the preoccupation with economic growth rates is viewed as a simple reflection of the way growth forms the very life-blood of the capitalist system and of its ability to survive. Capitalism, in all its varying guises, generates an internal dynamic in which individuals and governments are largely actors, following an elaborately worked script. In this way, colonialism and 'neo-colonialism' are seen as highly logical progressions in the evolution of capitalism on a world scale.

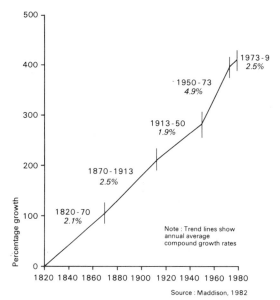

Figure 5.4 The capitalist core: growth of output (GDP at constant prices), 1820–1979

According to statistics compiled by Maddison (1982) and presented in Figure 5.4, the zenith of capitalist growth was achieved in the

90

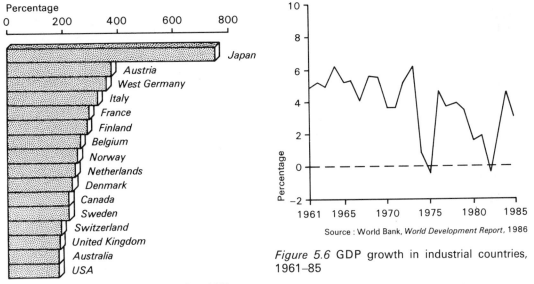

Percentage

Source : Maddison, 1982

Figure 5.5 The capitalist core: percentage increase in GDP per capita, 1950–79 (at 1970 US prices)

Source : World Bank, *World Development Report*, 1986

Figure 5.6 GDP growth in industrial countries, 1961–85

phase 1950–73. This was roughly double the rate achieved in the previous most successful phase (1870–1913). Japan, predictably, headed the list of sixteen core capitalist states, with an annual average compound growth rate of 9.7. The bar-chart (Figure 5.5) demonstrates the national breakdown of aggregate GDP* growth for these sixteen states over the slightly longer period of 1950–79. The relatively low positions of the UK and the USA testify to the penalties of being among the first industrial nations and to the competitive difficulties presented by the rise of new industrial states like Japan.

The year 1973 marked the first of the oil-price shocks and heralded a decade of uncertainty in economic growth in the industrialized world. Two major recessions, in 1973–5 and 1980–2, have resulted in a secular deceleration in growth rates over the period 1973 to 1985 and many commentators have pointed to the appearance of a longer-term

downward trend, as demonstrated, for instance, in the length and duration of 'troughs'. In some countries, the recessions brought negative values of national economic growth. In the UK in 1980 and 1981, for example, the annual percentage changes in GNP were − 2.6 and − 1.4. The USA in 1980 and 1982 recorded parallel values of − 0.2 and − 2.1.

* The World Bank defines GDP as 'the total final output of goods and services produced by an economy, regardless of the allocation to domestic and foreign claims'. As with GNP, no deductions are made for depreciation.

Rates of growth in the developing world

For countries of the Third World, the rate of economic growth is no less an objective than for the industrialized nations of the west. And given that absolute levels of GNP or GDP among undeveloped and developing nations are exceptionally low relative to the west, very much higher rates of GDP growth are necessary in order to achieve any measure of parallel progress. Thus one is faced with the otherwise curious paradox that annual rates of population growth of 2 or 3 per cent are viewed as disastrously high, but annual rates of economic growth of the same order are seen as disconcertingly low. Whereas in the industrial market economies between 1965 and 1973 the average annual rate of GDP growth was 4.7 per cent, among developing nations it was 6.6 per cent. Moreover, this figure hides a wide range of variation, with China and Brazil achieving figures of 7.8 and 9.6 per cent

respectively, while the low-income countries of Africa managed an average of only 3.9 per cent.

The relative level of GDP growth in the developing as against the industrial world over the period 1961–85 is depicted in Figure 5.7. Perhaps the most significant feature of the pattern of growth is its instability. There appears to be very limited capacity for sustained advance. In other words, the bases of economic growth are essentially fragile. The other clear feature of the pattern is the downward trend since the early 1970s. Over 1973 to 1980, the annual rate of GDP growth for all developing nations fell back from 6.6 per cent to 5.4 per cent; over 1981 to 1985 it dropped to 3.46 per cent. In the low-income countries of Africa, the corresponding figures were 3.9 to 2.7 and to 1.08 (see Figure 5.8).

Source : World Bank, *World Development Report*, 1986

Figure 5.7 Real growth of GDP, developing countries, 1961–85

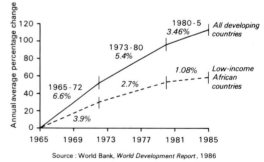

Source : World Bank, *World Development Report*, 1986

Figure 5.8 Trends in real growth of GDP, developing countries, 1961–85

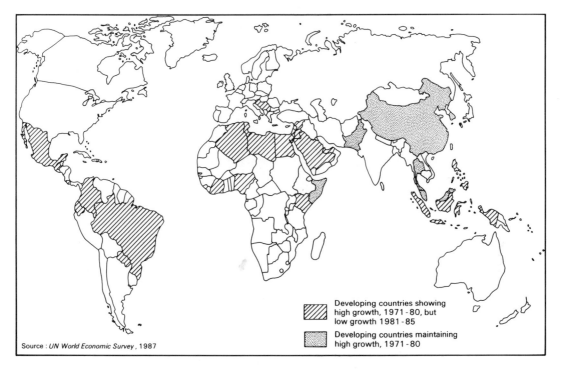

Figure 5.9 The caprices of economic growth in the developing world

The caprices of economic growth in the developing world over the two decades are represented in Figure 5.9. According to the UN, in the 1970s no fewer than 32 out of a sample of 80 developing countries could be classified as fast-growing, but by 1981–5 the number had shrunk to 14. No country of Latin America featured in the list of fast-growing states in the early 1980s, and only two figured from Africa (Cameroon and Congo). As the map indicates, sustained rapid growth appears to have become the monopoly of Southeast and East Asia, with the single exception of Oman. How far this reflects prevailing modes of political economy and the nature of production is not easily established. However, in the case of China the impact of domestic reform is inescapable, while such minor states as Hong Kong and Singapore might readily be cast more as integral to rather than peripheral to the developed industrial west.

The structure of production: agriculture

It has been conventional to see the development of manufacturing capacity as a key to the achievement of rapid economic growth. In this light, many developing countries, with their large agricultural sectors and diminutive manufacturing ones, are viewed as being seriously handicapped. And, when it is observed that there is a loose, inverse correlation between the percentage of GDP attributed to agriculture in developing countries and rates of economic growth, this interpretation is underlined.

Among industrial market economies in 1984, agriculture contributed an average of 3 per cent of GDP, as compared with 25 per cent for manufacturing. Among the low-income economies of sub-Saharan Africa, by contrast, agriculture contributed 39 per cent in 1984, whereas manufacturing contributed just 10 per cent. In the world's upper-middle-income economies, of which Brazil and Mexico are principal examples, the corresponding figures were 10 per cent and 25 per cent respectively. There is, in other words,

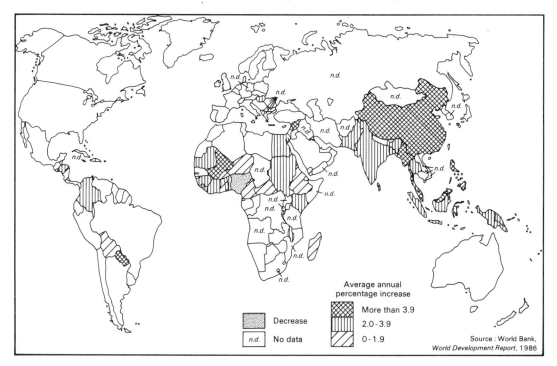

Figure 5.10 Growth in agricultural GDP, 1973–84 (among countries deriving 20 per cent or more of GDP from agriculture)

94

an enormous gulf between the structure of production of the poorer nations and that of nations of the industrial west or even their near economic allies. Moreover, signs of a major shift in this pattern are hard to discern. In the low-income economies of sub-Saharan Africa, the contribution of manufacturing to GDP grew by only one percentage point between 1965 and 1984, even if the proportion derived from agriculture contracted from 43 to 39 per cent.

It should not necessarily be assumed, of course, that Third World agriculture is inimical to sustained economic growth. In Burma, for example, one of the world's poorest nations in 1985 as measured in GNP per capita, the average annual increase in GDP between 1973 and 1984 was 6 per cent; and this in a country where agriculture accounted for 48 per cent of GDP in 1984. But as Figure 5.10 shows, few of the countries with substantial agricultural sectors exhibit strong rates of growth in agricultural GDP.

The expansion of agriculture in the developing world faces formidable obstacles; and this does not simply concern the sometimes difficult physical environmental conditions or the barriers of social practice. Because of the traditional importance attached to manufacturing growth by leading economic commentators, many Third World governments have pursued domestic agricultural policies which discriminate against the farming community, either directly through fiscal policy, or by default through the application of protective measures in industry. At the same time, and somewhat paradoxically, industrialized countries have instituted many measures of protection for their own agricultural

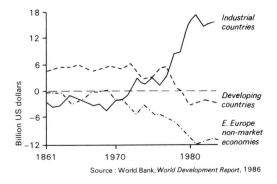

Source : World Bank, *World Development Report*, 1986

Figure 5.11 World food trade balance, 1961–84

sectors. The outcome is that an otherwise important arena of potential commodity exchange has been seriously diminished. If one examines the world's food trade balance since the early 1960s, the resulting effects are clearly apparent (see Figure 5.11). The developing world since 1970 has moved into a position of deficit, with imports outstripping exports by approximately 15 per cent in value terms by the early 1980s. Some of the growth in imports reflects positions where food demand has run ahead of supply or where the type of food demand has altered in a way that can be met only by imports from the industrial west (e.g. in the rising consumption of wheat); but much is due to the unfavourable terms of trade. In this respect, world agricultural development is hindered in a way that industrial development is not. The vigorous industrial growth in the states of East and Southeast Asia has been made possible through an open trading system, one relatively unfettered by tariffs and other impediments to free trade. In agriculture, no such free trade exists.

The structure of production: industry and services

Although it is still conventional to talk in terms of the *industrial* economies of the west, or of the world's *industrial* market economies, industry *per se* has long ceased to provide the major contribution to gross domestic product. That role has been assumed by the service sector, where by 1984 some 62 per cent of GDP in the industrial market economies was so derived. The proportion is slightly less if one takes employment as the structural indicator. In 1984, only 58 per cent of the total labour force was engaged in services. However, there was not a single country in the industrial west in 1984 that did not have the largest proportion of its labour force in the service industries. In the USA and Canada, in fact, 66 and 65 per cent respectively were in services. One has to go to the centrally planned economies of eastern Europe to find examples of developed nations in which the industrial sector retains economic dominance. Data here are very incomplete, but in Hungary and Poland in 1984 the contribution of industry to GDP was 42 and 52 per cent respectively. In employment terms, the average for all eastern European non-market economies in 1980 was 40 per cent in industry and 39 per cent in services.

The growth of the service sector in the western world has led to comment about the emergence of *post-industrial* economies. It remains true, however, that industry, and manufacturing in particular, despite declining shares of overall GDP output, continue to record significant rates of growth. For instance, over the crisis-ridden years of 1973–84, manufacturing in the industrial market economies grew by an average of 2.1 per cent per annum, as also did services. In the more prosperous phase, 1965–73, the corresponding percentage rates of growth were 5.3 and 4.8; and for Japan, understandably, the differential was infinitely more striking: 14.4 per cent against 8.3 per cent.

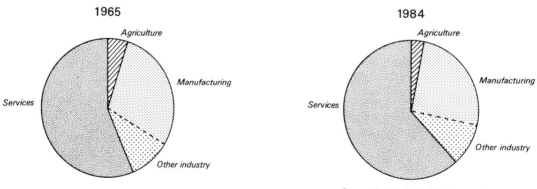

Source : World Bank, *World Development Report*, 1986

Figure 5.12 The structure of production in the industrial market economies (distribution of GDP)

If western-world development is taken as the model, growth of the service sector in the developing world would be expected to follow behind major expansions of the industrial or manufacturing base. In reality, of course, service growth has occurred ahead of or alongside industrial growth. In sub-Saharan Africa in 1984, whereas agriculture contributed 39 per cent of GDP, services contributed 43 per cent but industry a mere 18 per cent. In India, the corresponding figures for 1984 were 35 per cent agriculture, 27 per cent industry, and 38 per cent services. In China, though, the proportions in 1984 were 36 per cent for agriculture, 44 per cent for industry, and only 20 per cent for services. The Chinese pattern is one that is common for centrally planned economies where the 'consumer environment' is constricted in its growth by the economic apparatus of the state and where industrial expansion is a keystone of the Marxist-Leninist order. Even in the 'free' developing world, though, industrial growth has shown as much dynamism as growth in services. Among the world's low-income economies, for instance, industrial growth between 1965 and 1973 and between 1973 and 1984 averaged 8.9 per cent and 7.4 per cent respectively. The parallel rates for services were only 6.8 per cent and 5.0 per cent. Among the world's middle-income economies, the manufacturing sector recorded the highest rates of growth of any over the two periods 1965–73 and 1973–84 (9.2 per cent and 5.5 per cent). What this reflects of course, is the superficial nature of much service-sector activity in the developing world, allied only to domestic demand and often pre-industrial in its service type.

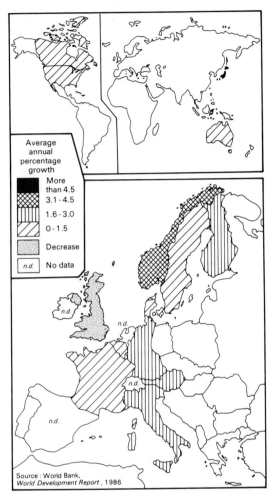

Source : World Bank, *World Development Report*, 1986

Figure 5.13 Industrial market economies: growth of industrial GDP, 1973–84

Debt

The phenomenon of national debt has become one of the most singular features of the world economic realm in recent decades. In 1985, the world's seven leading industrial countries were running budget deficits of between 1.4 and 13.1 per cent of their respective GNPs. Moreover, deficit budgets had been a feature of most of these states since 1979. In themselves, such deficits are not especially problematical. They may be met, for example, by higher domestic savings or by reductions in domestic public expenditure. However, if neither of these routes apply, the outcome is an influx of foreign capital, as occurred in the USA from the early 1980s. By 1985, for instance, some $113 billion of a budget deficit of $200 billion was financed by overseas investment. In response to this, the USA began to pursue a tight monetary policy which involved rising levels of interest rates. Given the importance of the USA in the economy of the western world generally, this had the effect of pushing interest rates up world-wide. High interest rates are not very conducive to business expansion in the developed economies; and for developing economies, with heavy borrowings already on record, the impact has sometimes been devastating.

Among all developing countries, the ratio of debt to GNP rose from 14.1 per cent in 1970 to 20.9 per cent in 1980 and then leapt to 33.8 in 1984. Among the low-income countries of Africa, the increase between 1970 and 1984 was from 17.5 per cent to 54.5 per cent; and the corresponding values for the ratio of debt to exports were 75.2 per cent and 278.1 per cent. For many developing economies, moreover, expansion of export capacity has been frustrated by trade protection in the west, so intensifying the debt cycle. The oil-price shocks of 1973–4 and 1979–80 have also contributed to the difficulties of sustained growth in GDP. By the same token, *declining* oil prices in the mid-1980s have had significant results for the developing oil economies, where previously buoyant revenues prompted governments to contract major investment loans which many now have difficulty in servicing. The outcome has been an intensive phase of debt rescheduling. This reached a record level of $93 billion in 1985. At the same time, many western financial institutions have begun to review their lending policies in the developing world: the economic environment has become too fragile to allow any major new release of long-term capital.

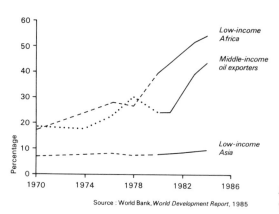

Source : World Bank, *World Development Report*, 1985

Figure 5.14 Ratio of debt to GNP in selected groups of developing countries

98

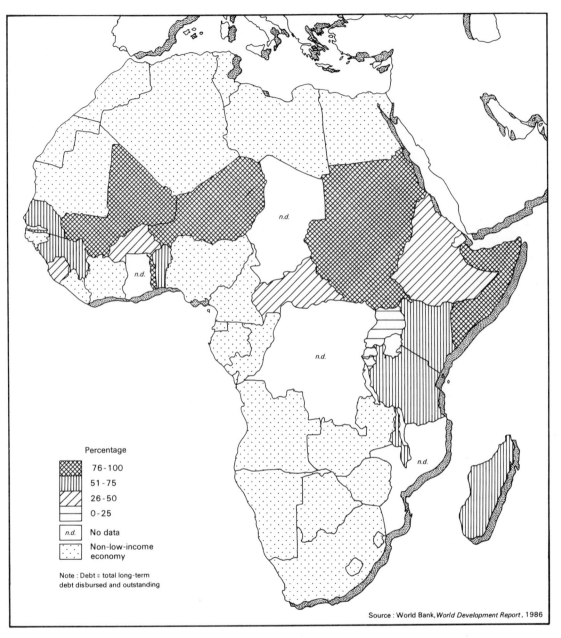

Figure 5.15 Africa: low-income economies: debt as a percentage of GNP, 1984

Foreign aid

The offering of grants and loans to countries of the developing world, particularly by members of the Organization for Economic Co-operation and Development (OECD) with its roots very firmly in the world's industrial market economies, has been a long-standing focus of debate and dissension. For some observers, development aid is seen as far too parsimonious relative to the wealth of the industrial west and the enormities of the problems in areas like sub-Saharan Africa. In 1985, for instance, OECD members provided grants and loans which amounted to just 0.36 per cent of their aggregate GNP. For the world's low-income economies, total development assistance received from OECD and other sources (e.g. OPEC) amounted to only 1.7 per cent of their aggregate GNP in 1984. *Within* these low-income economies, the countries of sub-Saharan Africa received development assistance in 1984 amounting to 9.0 per cent of their aggregate GNP. But even a figure of this order pales against the background of chronic indebtedness, runaway population growth, environmental deterioration, and civil strife which characterizes so many of them.

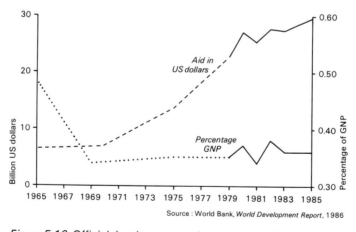

Source : World Bank, *World Development Report*, 1986

Figure 5.16 Official development assistance from OECD members, 1965–85

Over the twenty years from 1965 to 1985, development aid from OECD members has grown substantially, as Figure 5.16 reveals. As a percentage of GNP, however, it has shown stagnation and a tendency towards decline over the longer term. Moreover, member countries display marked variations in the scale of their commitment, as Figure 5.17 demonstrates. By 1984, the UK contribution was at its lowest percentage level for six years (0.33 per cent of GNP). Norway, by contrast, was then contributing 1.03 per cent of GNP, a near record level.

An entirely different view of development aid is that it is merely a supporting appendage to the process whereby the developed industrial world exploits the developing world through unbalanced terms of trade and other neo-colonial systems of resource development and transfer. Yet another approach is that which sees assistance as propping up unsatisfactory socio-economic systems and postponing vital structural reform; such aid thwarts indigenous development and stifles the 'pressure-response' mechanisms which are viewed by some as vital components in the internal dynamics of a society's progress. It is an exceptionally difficult task to proceed to a resolution of these differing views. And for Marxist commentators, anyway, this is ideologically unsound. What can be said is that aid has been accompanied by widely diverging outcomes; the contexts of capital assistance display great diversity, as do the results.

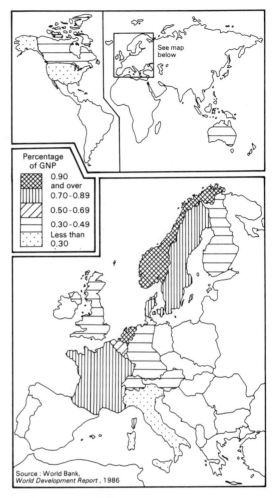

Figure 5.17 OECD development assistance, 1985 (by member country)

Liberian-registered tankers at the port of Southampton

6

Transport and trade

Railways

Shipping

Seaborne trade

Motor vehicles

Air transport

World merchandise trade

Railways

The 'world economy' was primarily a creation of the nineteenth century, even if European imperialism accorded it a character which the more modern forces of international capitalism have transformed if not destroyed. For many writers, the world economy of the nineteenth century was forged via the twin agencies of the railroad and the steamship; above all, the power of steam eroded much of the tyranny of distance; no longer was movement reliant upon wind and upon the muscle-power of the horse. W. W. Rostow viewed the railroad, in particular, as a major catalyst in the full-scale transition from pre-industrial to industrial society, especially among western nations like the United States and Britain. Not only did it widen and deepen markets, but it became a major consumer in its own right – notably from metal and engineering industries. In the continents of Africa and South America, the railroad was often in the frontline of resource development; in some cases it became the single most important medium of colonial administration and exploitation.

In the later twentieth century, the railroad has lost much of its former dominance, especially in the developed market economies. Although the USA has the longest railway system of any country in the world, it conveys little more than a third of the freight tonnage (measured in ton/km) of Soviet railways with a system only around three-quarters of the length. A rather similar contrast is apparent in any comparison of west European with east European states. East Germany, for instance, has a railway system less than half the size of that of West Germany and yet it carries 10 per cent more freight on a ton/km basis. France has the longest railway system of any European state, but the state which ranks highest in terms of freight traffic is Czechoslovakia, which operates a network only two-fifths the length of the French one.

Throughout the industrial market economies there has been a steady shift of freight traffic from rail to road. The generalization of the consumer market has exposed the weaknesses of rail alongside road transport; and

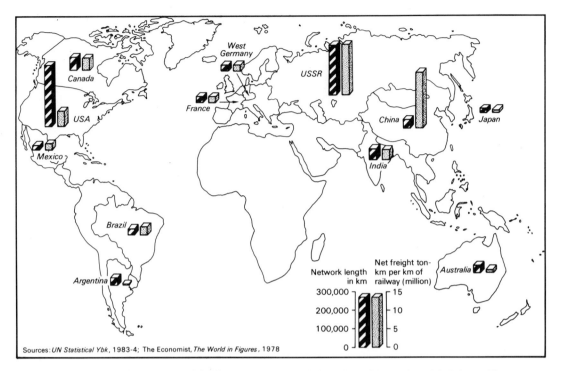

Figure 6.1 Principal world rail systems: network length and intensity of freight traffic

the relative freedom of the road sector from corporate control (public or private) has enhanced the resulting climate of competition. In the socialist block, by contrast, corporate control by the state has maintained the dominance of rail freight, although against the backcloth of less mature industrial economies, where consumer demand wields little control alongside the traditional sectors of industrial and manufacturing production.

In some of the industrial market economies, governments have sought to stabilize the split of freight haulage between road and rail by the provision of operating subsidies and various regulatory devices. In the UK, however, the volume of rail freight has collapsed on a scale unlike any other western state: the outcome of industrial and manufacturing decline, operating inefficiencies, and a government ideologically opposed to any form of state corporate organization.

Beyond the world's industrial market economies and the centrally planned economies of Europe (including the USSR), the role of railways in freight haulage is highly variable, although this has necessarily to be seen in the context of much lower levels of output relative to the industrial world. After North America and the USSR, India and China possess the longest railway systems, followed by Argentina and Australia. Asia, outside of the USSR, accounted for 13.5 per cent of total world rail freight in 1984 (measured in net ton/km). This was against 51 per cent for the USSR, 23.3 per cent for North America, and 8.5 per cent for Europe. Within Asia, Chinese rail freight in 1984 amounted to 722 billion net ton/km (c. 75 per cent of the Asia's total). For India, the parallel figure was 168 billion (17 per cent of the Asian total). As regards freight carriage, China now boasts the most intensively utilized rail system in the world, as Figure 6.1 reveals.

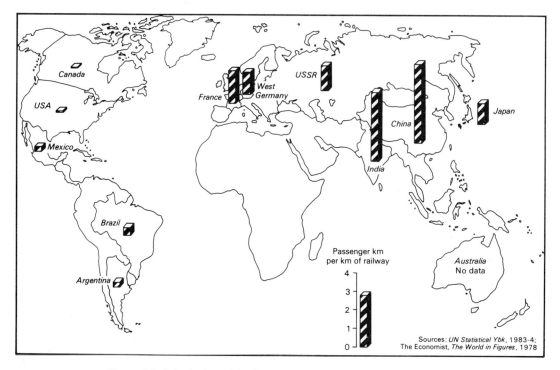

Figure 6.2 Principal world rail systems: intensity of passenger traffic

Railways have acted as formidable carriers of people as well as of goods. Indeed, in the UK in the early railway age, the volume of passenger traffic far outstripped expectations, with receipts even outrunning those from freight traffic for a time. Railways revolutionized the dynamic of commercial intercourse, especially in their alliance with the extension of the telegraph. They also helped to develop travel as a mass consumer good.

In the industrial market economies in the later twentieth century, rail passenger travel has become a shadow of its former state, the result of intense competition from automobile and aircraft. In the United States, the decades following the Second World War saw a dramatic collapse in railway passenger traffic. Over the 1980s, the pattern has been ameliorated somewhat, but in 1984 US railroads registered just 29.7 billion passenger kilometres, a figure almost identical to that of the UK in the same year. France, by contrast, recorded some 60 billion passenger kilometres, Poland some 53 billion. In the USSR, the figure for 1984 was 363 billion. Figure 6.2 relates rail passenger kilometres in 1984 to the lengths of national railway systems. The decline of North American rail passenger traffic is highlighted even more vividly by this criterion. By contrast, India and China emerge as having the most intensively used rail systems of all. The USSR, interestingly, is actually well behind the rest of Asia; even France boasted a greater intensity of passenger usage than the USSR.

In most of the industrial market economies, particularly those of Europe, it is the wide extension of personal car ownership that has dealt the death-blow to much rail passenger traffic. Over the past decade, however, as a result of increasing road congestion as well as deliberate government policies seeking oper-

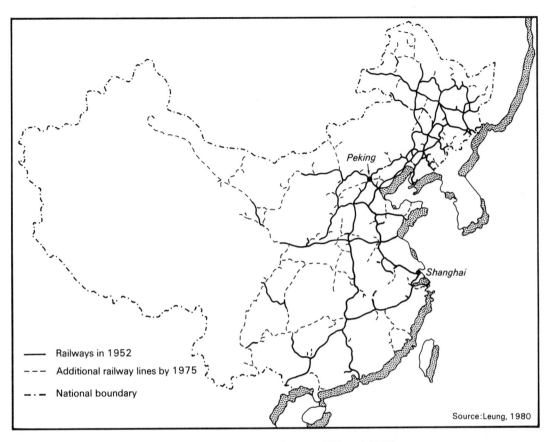

Figure 6.3 Railways in China, 1952 and 1975

ationally more efficient national transport systems, there has been a mild reversal of the downward spiral. In France, in particular, rail passenger usage was some 50 per cent higher in 1984 than in 1970, very largely as a result of large-scale investment in high-speed inter-city routes. Logically, one would expect the centrally planned economies of eastern Europe to show a greater intensity of rail pass-enger usage than in the west and little of the decline that has flowed from road competition. This is generally the case in reality, although Czechoslovakia and Hungary have each recorded secular reductions in traffic in recent years. Hungary, of course, has pursued what has been called market socialism and the change may legitimately be viewed in that light.

Shipping

The world's oceans and seas have provided a medium of transport since the beginning of civilization. The sea in fact represents a unique transport surface in terms of the way movement is unrestricted, except by winds and currents. It is also a remarkably frictionless medium alongside movement overland. Location theorists have coined the term *isotropic surface* to refer to spatial conditions where transport is free and easy in all directions: the sea comes close to that concept. This facet has been reflected, of course, in the way maritime states have in the past enhanced the bases of their political power. The Dutch,

Spanish, and Portuguese empires were rooted in maritime expansion. The British Empire perhaps represented the apotheosis of the pattern, particularly when one examines the British tramp-shipping business and the way it provided a pool of transport capacity which could be accessed almost upon demand: tramp steamers literally tramped the world in search of cargoes, representing a supremely logical response to the isotropic transport surface that the high seas presented to western man.

In the later twentieth century the high seas have become a vital lubricant of what has been called global capitalism. Although one could

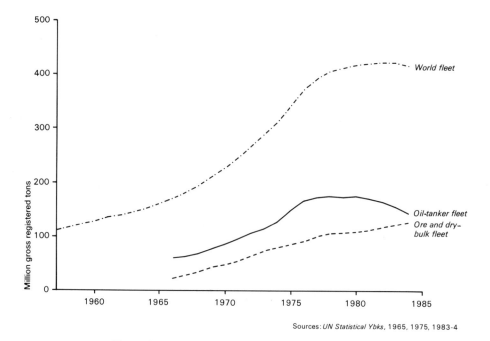

Sources: *UN Statistical Ybks*, 1965, 1975, 1983-4

Figure 6.4 World merchant-shipping fleet, 1957–85

talk of a world economy by the end of the nineteenth century, it was an economy that revolved around a few imperial monopolies, the British Empire among them. Today, however, the list of participants has grown considerably and the forces of capital have forged a more truly internationalist world realm. The world trade in crude oil is symptomatic of the trend, as also is the more recent growth in ore and dry-bulk trades. Advances in the technology of ship-building from the 1950s witnessed the dawn of the super oil-tanker, in which formidable economies of scale were accrued: the ore and bulk trades have been affected in tandem.

In 1948, the world's merchant-shipping fleet stood at 80.2 million gross registered tons. Up to the 1980s, there was a vigorous expansion of this capacity: by 1978, for instance, gross registered tonnage had reached 406 million. During the 1980s, however, stagnation has prevailed. Tonnage was only 418.6 million in 1984, having fallen in two successive years. This change naturally reflects the pattern of depression which has characterized the capitalist world economy in the most recent decade. It has been most visible in oil-tanker tonnage, where the years 1980–4 have witnessed a reduction in capacity from 175 million to 144.3 million. Not only has there been a fall in world oil production, resulting in a reduced demand for tanker transport, but several consuming countries have become major oil producers in their own right, destroying the *raison d'être* of some of the world's oil-tanker fleet. The pattern in ore and dry-bulk cargoes has been a more vigorous one. Over the years 1980–4, for example, tonnage rose from 109.5 million to 128.3 million. The growth in the international coal trade, consequent upon the oil-price shocks, naturally figures here; but in the world's leading metal industries, there is an ever-widening search for cheaper raw materials, for which the bulk-carrier fleets have become a vital enabling facility.

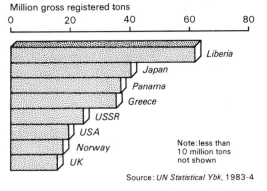

Million gross registered tons

Note: less than 10 million tons not shown

Source: *UN Statistical Ybk*, 1983-4

Figure 6.5 Flags of convenience, 1984

The use of statistics on gross registered tonnage is, of course, prone to misinterpretations. It cannot be assumed that this is a direct surrogate of the volume of maritime trade. At any one time, some fleet capacity may be under repair; since the mid-1970s there has been an increasing proportion of tonnage laid up. Similar sorts of difficulties arise over country of registration. The 'flags' under which merchant vessels operate are often an inadequate guide to ownership. Whilst the 40.3 million tons registered under Japan may reflect something of the strength of Japanese merchant-shipping interests, the 62 million registered under the Liberian flag do not, or only in a very marginal way. Much the same holds for the 37.2 million tons registered in Panama (see Figure 6.5). The rise of 'flags of convenience' reflects the desire of shipowners to maintain or improve their profit margins by searching out the states where the regulation of merchant shipping is most favourable to them; this applies especially in respect of labour conditions. That this is possible reflects, of course, the peculiar nature of marine transport in comparison with transport overland. Whereas states can achieve more or less exclusive regulation of the transport operations within their domain, the high seas present a free-for-all where the competitive machinery of capitalist ship-owning has untrammelled scope.

Seaborne trade

The geography of international sea trade is naturally a complex field, if only because of the enormous flexibility of movement that the high seas permit. The basic dimensions of the trade are illustrated in Figures 6.6 and 6.7, which depict the goods loaded and unloaded according to the eight main continental and sub-continental divisions, distinguishing oil from dry cargo. The maps say nothing of the origin–destination pattern; it would be exceedingly difficult to represent this cartographically at anything other than a simplified level. However, certain inferences may be made from the information displayed in the light of earlier discussions.

One of the most striking features of the maps is undoubtedly the diminutive scale of the USSR's maritime trade. In some measure, of course, this reflects its lack of maritime access; but it is also a function of a low level of external trade. As discussed earlier, however, the USSR *is* a significant oil exporter and this is readily apparent in the way roughly two-thirds of the tonnage of goods loaded in 1983 consisted of crude petroleum and petroleum product. The two maps also reveal

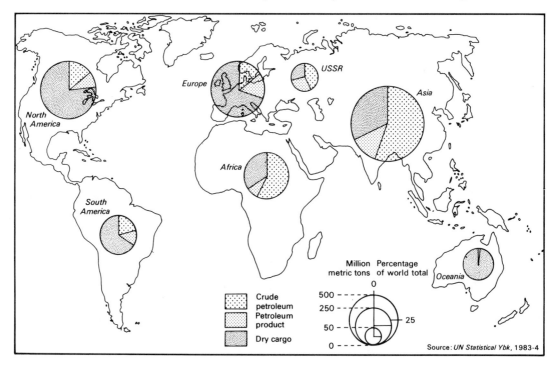

Figure 6.6 International seaborne freight in 1983: goods loaded

some quite startling imbalances between goods loaded and goods unloaded, i.e. between exports and imports. Europe is a particular case in point. The volume of goods unloaded was more than double the volume loaded. Measured simply in volumetric terms, therefore, and ignoring overland trade, Europe had an acute imbalance in 1983. Much of this consisted of oil imports: the net oil importation was some 407 million metric tons.

The opposite of this trade pattern is evident in the continents of Africa and South America: both were much more significant as exporters than as importers. To a considerable degree, of course, these trade imbalances are resolved when the basis of examination is value rather than volume. For instance, Europe can import a vastly greater tonnage than it exports because its imported goods are by and large cheaper than those it exports. The reverse naturally applies for Africa and South

America; and Australia also fits the latter pattern. It remains true, however, that for some countries of Africa and South America, trade positions are affected by biased *terms of trade* as much as trade composition.

Finally, one cannot examine these maps without being struck by the formidable place of oil in international seaborne trade. For North America, some 60 per cent of its goods *unloaded* consisted of crude petroleum or petroleum product; for Europe, the figure was near 50 per cent. For Asia and Africa, some two-thirds of their goods *loaded* consisted of petroleum. These features serve to underline the position of oil in the internationalization of capital. As the earlier statistics on the world's merchant fleet demonstrated, until the 1980s well over half the world's shipping capacity was devoted to oil carriage of one form or another.

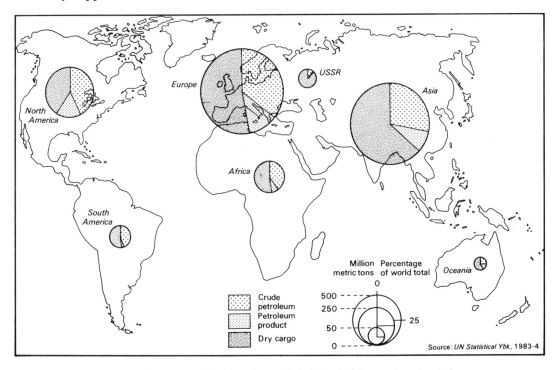

Figure 6.7 International seaborne freight in 1983: goods unloaded

Motor vehicles

The motor car has become one of the most distinctive hallmarks of modern western society. In American parlance, the twentieth century has become the age of the automobile in much the same way that the nineteenth century became the age of the railway. By the mid-twentieth century, automobile production had become one of the world's leading manufacturing sectors, so much so that governments have felt bound to intervene when companies appear to be failing. By contrast, in the socialist world, and in many lesser developed countries, the motor car's significance is considerably weaker. As a symbol of consumer capitalism, the car is clearly at variance with socialist goals and values. And in some socialist states, anyway, road networks are seriously deficient relative to their western counterparts. In less developed countries, although the motor car may be prominent in capital cities and their environs, general levels of per-capita income are so low as to make car ownership of very limited significance, quite apart from the more fundamental barriers of culture and a predominant agricultural peasantry.

These various contrasts are readily apparent in Figure 6.9. The USA alone accounted for 37 per cent of passenger cars in the world in 1982; West Germany and Italy claimed a further 7 per cent and 6 per cent respectively. In the USSR, however, the parallel figure was a diminutive 2.8 per cent; and for China just 0.07 per cent.

Since the end of the Second World War, motor-vehicle usage has expanded in relatively uninterrupted fashion, as Figure 6.8 reveals. In 1948, there were some 43 million cars in use in total, approximately 82 per cent of them found in North America, largely in the USA. By 1982 that figure had risen to some 342 million, with little sign of any slowing in growth. The USA no longer dominated to the same degree, but, as previously demonstrated, the car remains very much a western phenomenon. By 1983, for instance, Europe's market economies accounted for 33.7 per cent of the world total, having advanced from just 12 per cent in 1948.

Commercial-vehicle usage reveals a similar upward growth since the Second World War. The number of vehicle units rose from some

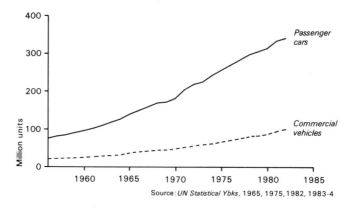

Source: *UN Statistical Ybks*, 1965, 1975, 1982, 1983-4

Figure 6.8 Motor vehicles in use, 1956–82

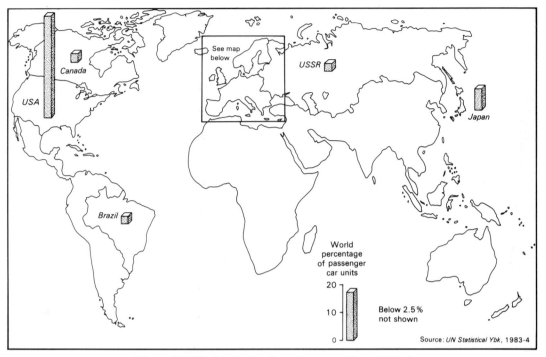

Figure 6.9 World distribution of automobiles, 1982-3

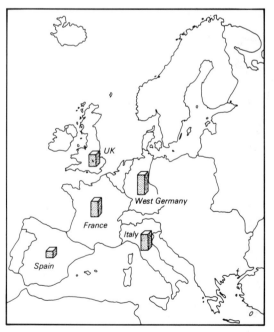

13 million in 1948 to around 100 million by 1982. The USA still dominates the pattern; in 1982, 35.6 per cent of all commercial vehicles in use were to be found in America. The USSR, by contrast, accounted for 8.3 per cent, roughly three times the equivalent figure for cars. And in countries like China and India, there were also proportionately more commercial vehicles. It remains true that, against a country like France, which had 2.9 per cent of the world's total in 1982, such figures are diminutive. But it must be remembered that in some of the lesser developed countries, rail freight enjoys a far greater importance than road freight. This is also true of the USSR and many of the states of the eastern bloc. Moreover, the Soviet Union has a road network which is less than a quarter of the length of that of the USA, so it is perhaps hardly surprising that it possesses less than a quarter of the USA's commercial-vehicle stock.

113

Air transport

Air is the most advanced of all the current forms of transport. And more than any of the other modal systems, it is dominated by the west. In 1984, the world's airlines recorded 1269.2 billion passenger kilometres, that is for all scheduled international and domestic services. North America accounted for 42.4 per cent of this total, the USA alone for 24.2 per cent. The continents of Africa, South America, and Oceania, by contrast, each registered 3 per cent or less. For Europe and Asia, the parallel figures were 17.4 and 17 per cent; the USSR accounted for 14 per cent of the passenger kilometres flown.

For the continental states of the world, air provides an important means of internal passenger transport. Thus one finds that 78.5 per cent of US passenger kilometres were recorded in domestic travel; for Canada the parallel figure was 53.6 per cent. The contrast is with small island nations such as the UK where only 5.6 per cent of passenger kilometres were generated domestically; for Switzerland the figure was a miniscule 1.8 per cent. In the case of states which are not major participants in the international capitalist economy, the ratio of domestic to international traffic is high, although geographical size remains a significant dimension. The USSR, for instance, generates 93.8 per cent of its air passenger kilometres internally; China 66.2 per cent. Romania and Yugoslavia, however, register figures of only 23 per cent and 20.7 per cent, an obvious reflection of their limited geographical capacity for internal air traffic.

Measured in passenger kilometres, the scale of air travel is remarkable when set alongside other modal systems. In 1984, for instance, US railroads registered 29.7 billion passenger kilometres, whereas for air traffic the corresponding figure was 479.2 billion. In the UK, the difference was much smaller: 30 billion rail passenger kilometres against 53 billion air passenger kilometres, although this has to be seen in the context of a very limited domestic demand for air travel. Measured only in numbers of passengers carried, of course, air travel pales into insignificance alongside rail travel. Air travel is, in other

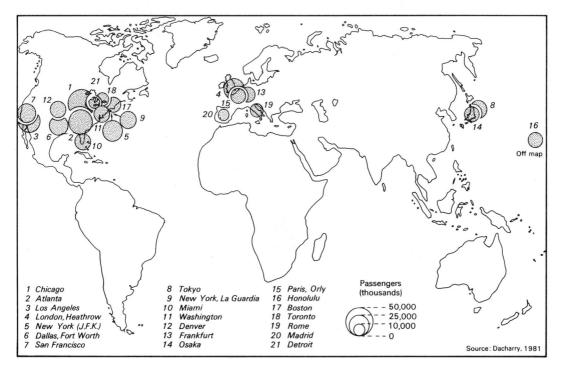

1	Chicago	8	Tokyo	15 Paris, Orly
2	Atlanta	9	New York, La Guardia	16 Honolulu
3	Los Angeles	10	Miami	17 Boston
4	London, Heathrow	11	Washington	18 Toronto
5	New York (J.F.K.)	12	Denver	19 Rome
6	Dallas, Fort Worth	13	Frankfurt	20 Madrid
7	San Francisco	14	Osaka	21 Detroit

Passengers (thousands)
- 50,000
- 25,000
- 10,000
- 0

Source: Dacharry, 1981

Figure 6.10 Passenger traffic at major world airports, 1978

words, confined to a very restricted element of the world's population. This is explained largely by price factors and by the high mean distance of most air journeys. It may well be that, in the west, the dawn of cheap foreign-holiday 'packages' has opened up air travel to a much wider mass of society, but this is an ephemeral rather than a regular traffic. For very large sectors of the world's populus, air travel remains remote from everyday experience.

Air travel has had nothing like the same impact on freight movement as it has had in the passenger realm. The world total for air freight movement in 1984 was 39.3 billion ton/km; for rail freight it was 7,142 billion. Whether it is for domestic or international traffic, air freight is highly uncompetitive in price, the exceptions being materials of very high value in relation to their bulk or weight and materials which are of relatively high value but perishable. Precision instruments are an example of the former, fresh exotic fruits of the latter. Some 25.8 per cent of world air freight kilometres in 1984 were attributable to the USA. Europe and North America together contributed 57.4 per cent. There remains, however, one sector of air freight where tonnage figures belie its importance. The sector is mail traffic. The development of air-mail services from the 1930s became an important agency of the internationalization of the world economy. And, in some cases, mail contracts became the datum from which passenger services were organized, particularly up to the Second World War. In the 1980s, of course, electronic mailing methods are beginning to compete with the traditional mail traffics, although this is within the realm of a continuously expanding market. Between 1975 and 1984, for example, total mail ton/km rose from 1.72 billion to 2.49 billion.

World merchandise trade

Merchandise refers to international movements of goods across customs borders; it encompasses primary as well as manufactured commodities. Between the periods 1965–73 and 1973–84, the merchandise trade of the world's low-income economies grew (by value) from an average rate of 0.25 per cent per annum to 5.2 per cent per annum. And yet, as Figure 6.13 reveals, the low-income economies still accounted for only a minute proportion of the world's merchandise trade in 1984: about 3 per cent. Instead, it is the nineteen industrial market economies which command the bulk of the world merchandise trade (65.6 per cent in 1984). Moreover, if one analyses the destinations of merchandise exports for the industrial market economies (see Figure 6.12), it is apparent that much of their trade is internal, i.e. among themselves. In 1984 the percentage figure was 70; in 1965 it was 71, reflecting remarkably little change over twenty years.

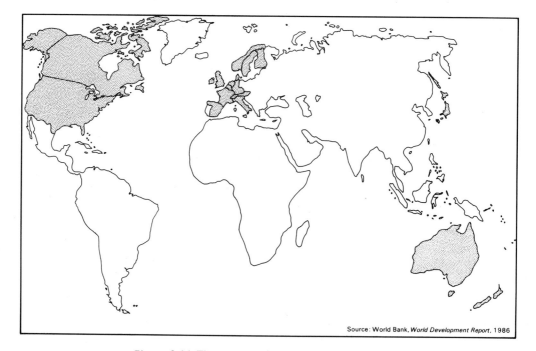

Source: World Bank, *World Development Report*, 1986

Figure 6.11 The world's industrial market economies

116

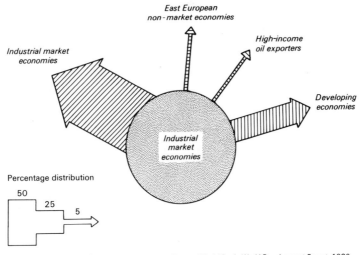

Source: World Bank, *World Development Report*, 1986

Figure 6.12 Industrial market economies: destination of merchandise exports in 1984

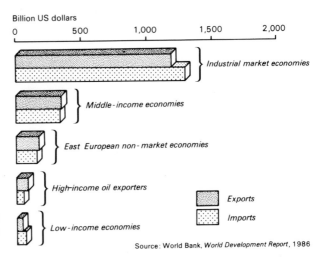

Figure 6.13 Merchandise trade in 1984 (according to the World Bank's economic classification)

Source: World Bank, *World Development Report*, 1986

By the same token, if one examines merchandise exports for the low-income economies (Figure 6.16), it emerges that half of them went to the industrial market economies in 1984. The parallel figure for the world's middle-income economies in 1984 was even higher: 64 per cent (see Figure 6.15). Thus there appear to be strong asymmetric elements to the world's merchandise trade; while commodities flow from the *developing* economies to the *developed* economies – the so-called capitalist core – there is limited reciprocal movement. In 1984, only 24 per cent of the merchandise exports of the industrial market economies went to the developing countries (that is low-income and middle-income economies); in 1965 the figure had actually been higher: 26 per cent.

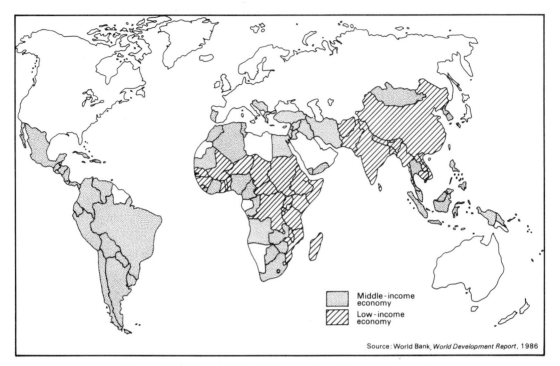

Source: World Bank, *World Development Report*, 1986

Figure 6.14 The world's middle- and low-income economies

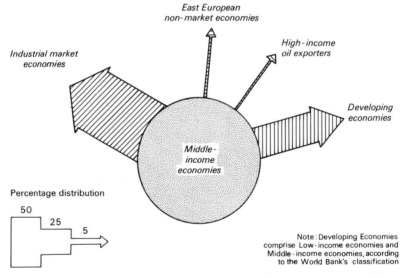

Note: Developing Economies comprise Low-income economies and Middle-income economies, according to the World Bank's classification

Source: World Bank, *World Development Report*, 1986

Figure 6.15 Middle-income economies: destination of merchandise exports in 1984

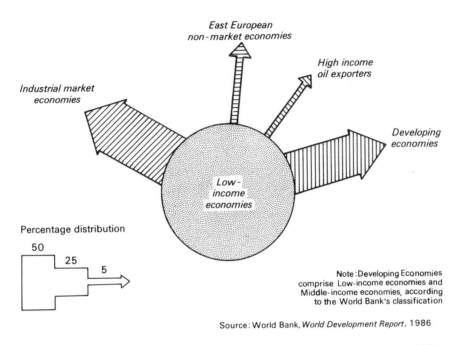

East European
non-market economies

High income
oil exporters

Industrial market
economies

Developing
economies

Low-
income
economies

Percentage distribution

50

25

5

Note : Developing Economies
comprise Low-income economies and
Middle-income economies, according
to the World Bank's classification

Source: World Bank, *World Development Report*, 1986

Figure 6.16 Low-income economies: destination of merchandise exports in 1984

To some extent, however, the preceding statistics are misleading. If one begins to look at the actual values rather than percentages, it is clear that the developing economies receive rather more from the industrial market economies than they trade in return. For 1984, the results were 287 million and 252 million US dollars respectively, giving a clear trade imbalance. The outcome, therefore, is something of a double-edged sword. The developing economies rely on the industrial market economies for a very substantial proportion of their export markets, but for the industrial market economies this forms a very minor part of their import commitment and hence is relatively invulnerable to bargaining. In much the same way, the developing economies face a heavy import bill for merchandise from the industrial market economies, and yet this accounts for a relatively small proportion of the total exports of the industrial market economies, where a great deal of export trading is internal. Thus the developing economies are in a potentially serious position of dependency relative to the industrial market economies. How far this potential has been realized is much debated; the precise mechanisms of dependency are also disputed. An important sign of change, however, has been the increasing degree to which the developing economies are trading among themselves. For the low-income economies, for instance, the percentage of merchandise exports in this category rose from 32 to 40 between 1965 and 1984. For the middle-income economies, the parallel change was from 23 to 31. This is undoubtedly a shift to a more fragile marketplace, but the dependency connotations are fewer.

119

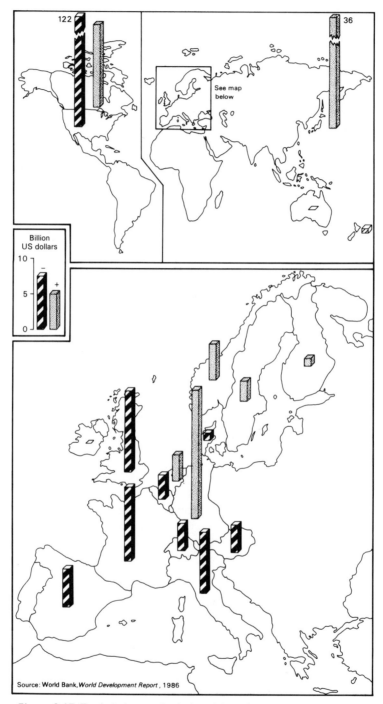

Figure 6.17 Trade balances for industrial market economies in 1984

The dominating economic position of the industrial market economies in the world's merchandise trade is slightly overshadowed when one examines the visible trade balances. In 1984, imports exceeded exports by 92 billion dollars, as Figure 6.13 demonstrated. However, when invisible trade is considered as well, the position alongside other income groupings sharpens again; for the financial, insurance, and other service sectors are realms in which states outside the west play remarkably little part. Of course, when the performance of the industrial market economies is disaggregrated, the picture becomes much more diverse. In 1984, for instance, eleven out of the nineteen industrial market economies showed visible trade imbalances. The USA was the most significant member of this group with an import bill of 338 billion dollars against export earnings of 216 billion. Japan, by contrast, registered imports to the value of 134 billion US dollars, but exports of 170 billion. If such a range of trade deficits appears serious at first sight, it should be remembered that many of the states concerned record sizeable trade earnings from invisibles.

It has become a matter of some debate as to how far the economies of eastern Europe (including the USSR) are part of the *world economic system* or feature in what has been called *world accumulation*. It was shown earlier how the USSR makes exports of oil and gas to the west in order to obtain vital foreign currency to meet, among other things, its recurrent problem of food deficits. However, the preceding charts demonstrate very clearly that the socialist bloc is an exceptionally limited recipient of other states' exports. Indeed, the value of its total merchandise trade in 1984 was minute relative to the industrial west; and this included trade among the socialist states themselves. Given the scale of industrial production in the socialist bloc and its economic status relative to the developing world, it is difficult to avoid the conclusion that most of the states of eastern Europe and the USSR exist in economic isolation alongside the other states of the developed world and the states of the developing world. This is not in any sense to deny the forces they have represented in the historical evolution of capitalism, but they contribute little to our understanding of how the contemporary world economy works.

Migrant labourers at work on the ship-breaking beach at Gadani, Pakistan

7
Labour

The relations of labour

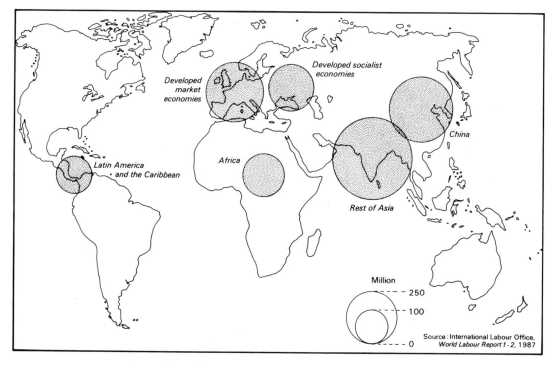

Figure 7.1 The world's labour force in 1980

If size of labour force were a direct guide to national wealth, the countries of South and East Asia would be among the richest in the world. This is not the case, of course. And what is especially remarkable about this map is the diminutive scale of the labour force of all the developed market economies put together. The wealth of the western world clearly derives from very different bases.

As long as mankind pursued a largely primitive life-style, one where self-sufficiency was the central determinant of human activity, the issue of labour was of limited secular significance. However, one of the hallmarks of the progress of civilization has been the increasing substitution of self-sufficiency by exchange, and, as part of this, the emergence of man as a seller of labour. Thus the issue of labour has become a critical dimension of the geographical environment.

The particular form of labour relations between buyer and seller is, of course, highly variable. On the one hand, there is the familiar example of the contract between factory-hand and factory-owner in which the hand performs a defined labour service. On the other, there is the less familiar example of the share-cropper who labours for himself but whose contract involves the passing on of a proportion of his crop to the landowner as land rent. Producer co-operatives provide yet a further variant: here it is the contractual obligation among producers which represents the key to labour relations rather than the more singular buyer–seller format. Leaving primitive peoples aside, some human activity is nevertheless performed which involves no contractual obligation in the way described above. This applies to the self-employed; it also relates to labour which is carried out as part of a family-livelihood setting.

In the industrial market economies and in the industrialized socialist world (i.e. east European non-market economies), simple wage-employment predominates. In the industrialized west this is hardly surprising given the way it was in the forefront of capitalist development; in the industrialized socialist states, it is a pattern which springs directly from political ideology, one where labour power is automatically in the harness of the state, although states like Hungary have begun to deviate somewhat from this pattern. In the industrialized west, self-employment has become an increasingly significant phenomenon, but in 1980 it still accounted for less than a quarter of all workers. In the developing world, of course, 'family workers' assume considerably more importance, as do the self-employed. In the former case, they constituted between about 10 and 25 per cent of the workforce in 1980; in the latter between 25 and 50 per cent.

The structure of the labour force

The structure of the world's labour force in 1980 is demonstrated in Figure 7.2, distinguishing the five income groupings used by the World Bank. The percentage of the population of working age (that is 15–64 years) varies from 55 per cent in the high-income oil exporters to 67 per cent in the industrial market economies. This represented a significant change over the pattern fifteen years earlier, in 1965, when the corresponding figures were 52 per cent and 63 per cent. Indeed, over that time-span, each of the five major income groups of the world's states registered a percentage growth in their labour forces. In the industrial market economies and in the industrialized socialist economies, this reflects the slowing of the birth rate, particularly in the wake of the post-war baby-booms; and in some cases (as demonstrated in an earlier section) population change is at or even below replacement rate. In the world's developing economies, the increase in the labour force is also a function of a slowing birth rate, although at a fundamentally higher level. In China, where population-control programmes have been operative since 1971, the percentage of the population of working age jumped from 55 to 64 per cent between 1965 and 1980. In India, by contrast, it rose only from 54 to 56.

The total world's population that is of working age and the total world labour force are not, in fact, quite the same thing. The latter includes all persons who are economically active above the age of ten; and this is especially relevant in many parts of the developing world. The basic divisions of the world's labour force, retaining the World Bank's income groupings, are depicted in the diagram. As previously indicated, it has been conventional to think of the proportions engaged in the agricultural, industrial and service sectors as indicative of distinctive levels of socio-economic development. Thus, a large agricultural labour force is reflective of a pre-industrial society, a large industrial labour force of an industrial society, and a large service sector of a post-industrial society. The industrial market economies fit the pattern fairly well when their historical records over the past 200 years are examined. The non-market economies of eastern Europe provide some semblance of the same sequence, except that the industrial and service sectors had arrived at a position of parity by 1980. This is an undoubted reflection of the restrictive nature of the prevailing political-economic systems as far as the provision of services goes; it also stems from lower levels of income. In the developing economies in 1980, however, the sequence followed in the industrialized world is largely confounded. In both the middle-income economies and the high-income oil exporters, the service sectors are larger than the industrial sectors, while the agricultural sectors remain larger than the industrial ones. The low-income economies do not present as confusing a pattern because such a large proportion of their labour force is in agriculture (70 per cent in 1980); but with 15 per cent of the labour force in services as well as in industry, the picture remains aberrant.

Labour

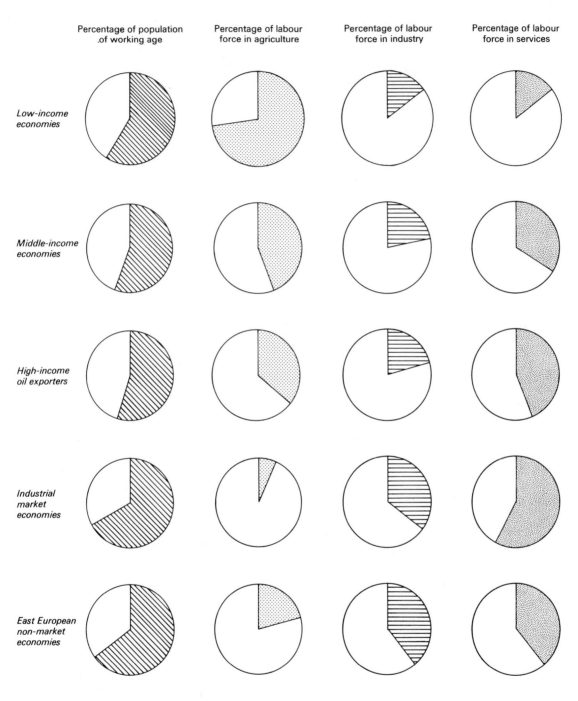

Figure 7.2 The structure of the world's labour force in 1980

Source : World Bank, *World Development Report*, 1986

The structure of the labour force: developing countries

It is possible to break down the results for the developing world by distinguishing continental and sub-continental areas. The outcome is depicted in Figure 7.3. China is the single realm which deviates from the general pattern of the developing economies. In 1980, 60 per cent of its labour was in agriculture, 25.8 per cent in industry, and 14.2 per cent in services. Otherwise, the data reveal that the service sector is everywhere dominant over industry; and in the middle-income econ-omies of Latin America and the Caribbean it even exceeds agriculture in significance. For that particular economic-geographical group-ing, agriculture in 1980 accounted for 31.8 per cent, industry 25.8 per cent, but services 42.4 per cent. If one extends the analysis back to 1965, it becomes clear that the pattern described in 1980 had little novelty about it. China again provided the single exception; otherwise the service sector still dominated the industrial one.

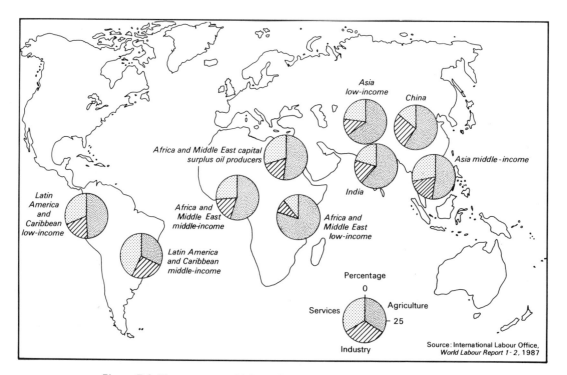

Figure 7.3 The structure of labour force in developing countries, 1980

The rapid rise of service employment in the developing world cannot, of course, be seen as indicative of an advanced level of socio-economic development. In this sense, the service sector in developing economies has grown in counterfeit fashion. In the industrialized world, service employment is rooted in the realms of investment, banking, insurance, wholesaling, and retailing; in the developing world, service activities are much more superficial. The 'shoe-shine' syndrome may be an overplayed one, but it is nevertheless symptomatic of the fragile basis of much service activity in developing countries. And one especially distinctive feature is the importance of domestic service – on the kind of scale that was characteristic of later nineteenth-century Europe. Much of this growth in service employment stems from the pressure of population, especially in rural environments. Large-scale rural out-migration has resulted in a burgeoning expansion of urban populations, but with a restrictive basis of economic support. Within this context, service-sector growth has represented what might be called 'the art of the possible'. That is not to say that industrial employment has not been growing – in all developing countries between 1960 and 1980, it grew from 12.8 per cent of the labour force to 19.9 per cent; but this has been inadequate to sustain the escalating pool of urban labour. And one of the 'drawbacks' of modern industrial employment, anyway, is its increasingly capital- rather than labour-intensive character. The ability of industry to act as sump for rural migrants, following the pattern of nineteenth-century Europe, has been sharply reduced. By contrast, service-sector employment is, almost by definition, labour-intensive.

Unemployment

In 1983, unemployment in the industrial market economies was at around 10 per cent of the total labour force. In real terms, this meant that some 35 million people were without jobs. And when set against the years of relatively full employment from the Second World War until the 1973 oil crisis, this has represented a bleak prospect. However, it is less bleak than the economic catastrophe of the 1930s, when in the USA nearly 13 million were out of work (about one worker in four). Germany suffered even more, with 6 million unemployed in 1932, or one worker in three.

The phenomenon of unemployment is very much related to the rise of wage-employment. Friedrich Engels, in his *Condition of the Working Class in England in 1844*, registered something of the force of unemployment which prevailed during the chronic depression years of the early 1840s and argued that it was a permanent, innate feature of the prevailing economic system. Thus has the concept of the 'industrial reserve army' become an established feature of Marxist thinking. In the twentieth century, western governments responded to the chronic unemployment of the Depression by interventionist economic measures. In parallel, various measures of collective social security were instituted to handle the social plight of the unemployed. The Cambridge economist J. M. Keynes, whose work contributed to the development of the interventionist approach, soon found himself the founder of a new kind of economics, labelled *Keynesian*. This was in contrast to the free-market economics of Adam Smith and Ricardo of more than a century before.

In the later 1970s and 1980s, the ability to apply Keynesian solutions to the western economies appears to have faded. Triggered by the dual oil-price shocks of 1973–4 and 1979–80, by the rapid economic rise of Japan, and by the emergence of strong manufacturing bases beyond the traditional western arena, rates of economic growth in the core states of the west had fallen to around zero by the early 1980s and unemployment reappeared on a scale unknown since the 1930s. Figure 7.4 illustrates the pattern of unemployment growth for fifteen OECD countries from 1974 to 1982. The definition of unemployment is much open to interpretation and a great deal of published data is not really capable of international comparison. However, the two charts are the outcome of careful statistical adjustment by OECD statisticians and record persons above a specified age who, during a defined period, were without employment, were currently available for employment, and were seeking employment. Taking the major states of OECD (Figure 7.4a), the scale of unemployment growth is readily apparent. The one state which has proved able to swim against the tide has been Japan – in substantial part a reflection of the way it has been a reciprocal of unemployment generation in other member states through extremely successful industrial competition. The United Kingdom's unemployment problem has undeniably been the most formidable of the leading industrial market economies. Standing at around only 3 per cent in 1973/4, it had reached 13 per cent by 1982/3.

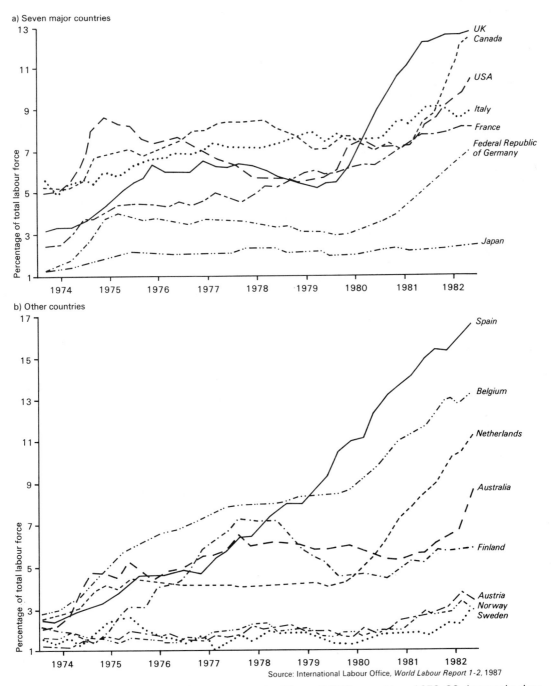

Source: International Labour Office, *World Labour Report 1-2*, 1987

Figure 7.4 Standardized unemployment rates in fifteen OECD countries, 1972–83 (quarterly data seasonally adjusted)

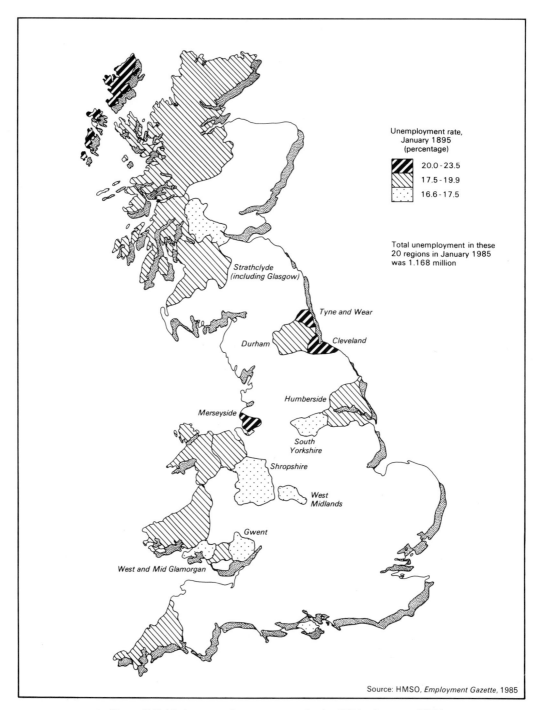

Figure 7.5 High-unemployment areas in the UK in January 1985

One of the things that distinguishes the economic problems of the 1980s from those of the 1930s is the greatly increased internationalization of the economic system. This is not simply a question of the rise of new competitors and of their infiltrating markets, but it refers to the way single state governments enjoy a much reduced level of control over their own destinies. Some countries, the UK among them, have undoubtedly had their tasks complicated by major structural weaknesses. At a broader level, there has also been a perceptual problem over the way the major economies of the world are in the throes of fundamental transformation; it has been easier to retain the belief that the current difficulties are merely fluctuations along a familiar track.

A seeming paradox of the current unemployment problem is the fact that, in OECD countries between 1960 and 1980, the labour force benefited from a net increase of 65 million jobs. In fact, the numbers in civilian employment grew at an average annual rate of 1.1 per cent. The apparent paradox is explained, of course, by growing numbers of people coming on to the employment market and by the way new jobs have increasingly been taken up not by those being laid off but by newcomers to the labour market. The dramatic increase in female participation rates in many OECD countries, provides a specific illustration. Of similar importance, though, has been the expansion of the youth labour force from the 1970s – as the children born in the post-war baby-boom came of working age.

Unemployment is not a phenomenon that is uniformly distributed, either geographically, or through the various dimensions of the social strata. In the United States in 1980, for example, white youth recorded an unemployment rate of 16.2 per cent male and 14.8 per cent female; for black youth, however, the corresponding rates were 37.4 per cent and 39.9 per cent. And the pattern was no less distinct, if less marked, in 1960. Among ten OECD countries in 1981, unemployment rates for women were 7.3 per cent, while for men they were 4.98 per cent. In the Federal Republic of Germany the female rate in 1981 was 14.2 per cent against a male rate of only 5.3.

It is in the geography of unemployment, though, that some of the sharpest inequalities have become exposed. This has been especially acute in the United Kingdom, with its many densely populated old industrial regions. Such areas of large-scale specialization in heavy branches of industry, their evolution often closely tied towards Empire markets, have proved pathological features in the industrial climate of the twentieth century and against the increasing internationalization of capital. Figure 7.5 depicts the unemployment rates in January 1985 for the twenty counties/regions of the UK recording the highest totals. They were headed by Cleveland on Teesside, with 23.5 per cent, although the West Midlands (16.8 per cent) actually presented the highest absolute value: 221,246 persons. The unemployment problem is not seen at its most serious, though, until one examines the intra-regional scale. Within Glasgow, for instance, Bridgeton/ Dalmarnock registered a *male* unemployment rate of 50.8 per cent in January 1985, with an average male rate for the city as a whole of 27.4 per cent.

Perhaps one of the most disturbing features of unemployment in the industrial market economies by the 1980s has been the growth of the long-term unemployed. Here, the concept of the 'reserve army' appears to lose much of its force, for this is a labour group where the trades of which they were part are rapidly disappearing – either through material substitution or through spatial displacement to other parts of the world. The pattern is exacerbated where the labour pools concerned are found in what are today relatively peripheral economic regions: the major foci of nineteenth-century industrial development are not generally the same as in the twentieth,

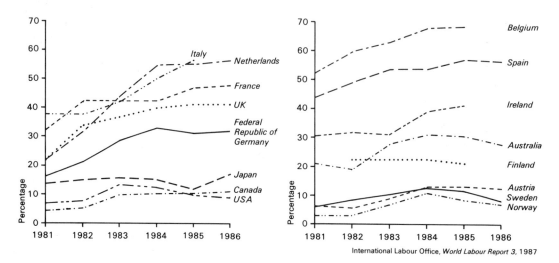

International Labour Office, *World Labour Report 3*, 1987

Figure 7.6 Percentage of the unemployed out of work for over one year: industrialized market economies, 1981–6

so that there arises an increasing mismatch between the geography of residual labour groups and the geography of new employment. The growth of the long-term unemployed in the industrial market economies between 1981 and 1986 is demonstrated in Figure 7.6. A high mobility of labour is clearly one key to the problem. This is a particular characteristic of the North American labour force and hence its rates for long-term unemployed are lower. Even so, mobility does nothing for the simple fact of a net shortfall in employment over a continuing time-span.

Unemployment is not, of course, confined to the developed world. Where developing countries have experienced a growth in wage-employment, especially in the urban sector, unemployment has become apparent, if not always for the same sets of reasons. However, to find statistics on unemployment which may be compared with the industrial market economies is exceptionally difficult. And given the much higher percentage of the labour force which is self-employed or working in the context of the family, it is anyway questionable how far such a comparison

would be justified. Another common attribute of the labour force in developing countries is the existence of *under-employment* as distinct from unemployment. In the Asian economies, for instance, it has been estimated that some 40 per cent of the labour force in rural areas may fall into this category.

Figure 7.7 sets out the unemployment rate for various countries in 1985, but omitting Asia and Africa altogether, given the data problems and the questions over applicability. Yet even a cursory glance at the pattern reveals continuing deficiencies in the data. Some countries of South America, for example, register rates considerably below those of industrial Europe. Mexico provides a particular case in point, as does Argentina. Beyond this, one cannot fail to be struck by Japan's minimal 2.6 per cent unemployed. The low figures for South Korea and Hong Kong echo the pattern. These states of the eastern Pacific rim have succeeded in developing vigorous new manufacturing bases which have stolen a march on many of the traditional producers in the industrial west.

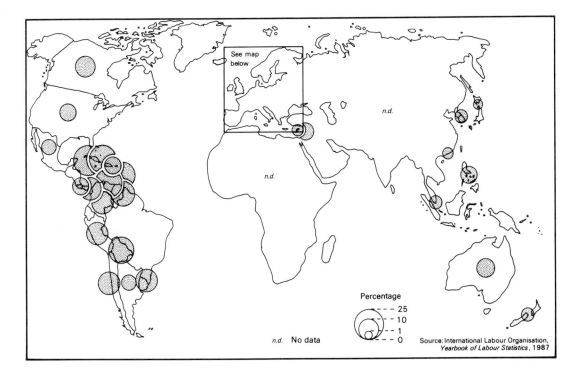

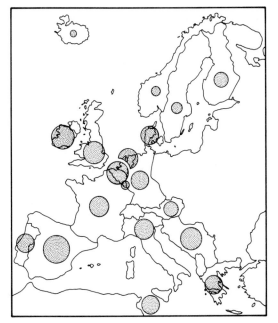

Figure 7.7 The rate of unemployment in various countries in 1985

Women

In the industrialized west in the second half of the twentieth century, the role of women in economy and society has altered considerably. As average family size has contracted, as the number of childless couples has grown, as divorce has increased, and as inequality of the sexes has become the focus for debate, so female participation rates have grown and likewise the percentage of the labour force represented by women. The housewife-and-mother stereotype became stigmatized in many quarters, and, coupled with the social trends which have undermined the traditions of the family, society at large has accommodated to a very different outlook on the woman's role.

Outside the industrial west, of course, women have typically fulfilled a much more prominent role, especially in agriculture. In the industrialized socialist world, moreover, women have been found in a far greater range of employment than in the industrial west, often embracing manufacturing sectors which, in western countries have long been exclusive male domains. By about 1980, in fact, eastern Europe and the USSR had the highest rates of female participation of all the world's principal socio-economic groupings. In the case of developing countries, the labour performed by women has necessarily to be seen in the context of the family, as part of a family-livelihood system where money-related notions of labour are inappropriate. In some developing countries, though, religious belief decrees a very limited role for women.

Figure 7.8 indicates the scale of female participation rates in sixteen OECD states around 1976. This applies to women of ages 15 to 64.

From 1950 to 1976 the aggregate increase in participation rates was from 38.1 per cent to 50 per cent, but showing a wide variation. Australia's percentage, for example, jumped from 29.5 to 49.6, whereas that for Austria remained virtually stable around 47. However, these changes cannot be taken entirely at face value. The statistics for 1950 hide significant variation in statistical convention, particularly over the counting of female agricultural labour. This does not invalidate the *trends* revealed (especially given the progressive diminution in agricultural labour, generally, in the post-war decades), but it requires that the precise scale of change be viewed with caution. Such a qualification does not apply to the participation rates for 1976 mapped here on a country-by-country basis; from the mid-1950s labour surveys such as these have become standardized across most OECD countries. Sweden had the highest participation rate in 1976 (67.7 per cent); indeed, Scandinavia, generally, revealed a mean of 62.6 per cent, against a mean for all sixteen states of 50 per cent. Italy, with a participation rate of 30.8 per cent, was the lowest of the sixteen. The equivalent male participation rate for all sixteen states in 1976 was 84 per cent.

By 1980, according to OECD sources, the female participation rate for fifteen member states had risen to 52.1 per cent against a corresponding male figure of 85.5 per cent. And Scandinavia remained at the forefront of 'female emancipation': for Sweden the female rate had reached 74.1 per cent in 1980, against a male rate of 87.8.

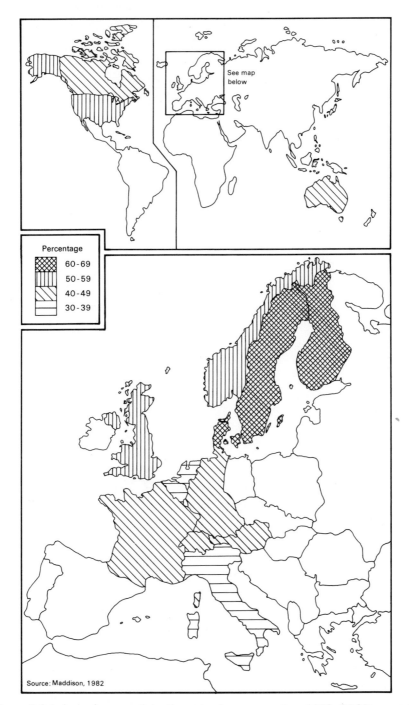

Figure 7.8 Labour-force participation rates for women circa 1976, OECD countries

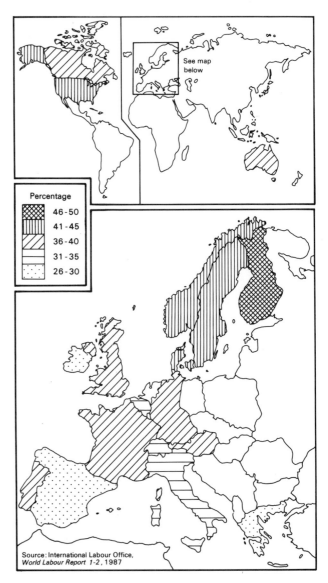

Figure 7.9 Women as a percentage of employed labour force in 1981, OECD countries

Source: International Labour Office, *World Labour Report 1-2*, 1987

One may also consider women in terms of the percentage of the employed labour force that they represent. Figure 7.9 sets out the figures for a wide range of OECD states for the year 1981. The average was 38.6 per cent, with Finland at the top of the range on 47.6 per cent and Ireland at the bottom on 28.5 per cent. These figures are broadly consistent with those on participation rates. Moreover, if the time-scale is extended – back to 1960, for example – the same rising trend of female employment is clearly apparent: in that year, some 34.3 per cent of the employed labour force consisted of women.

One of the most important facets of the growth of female employment has been its increasingly part-time form. Part-time employment, generally, has grown considerably since the first 1970s recession and is clearly in part a direct symptom of economic uncertainty. In the UK in 1981, some 20 per cent of all employment was part-time; and in most other industrial market economies it exceeds 10 per cent. The proportion of part-time work taken up by women is high and is increasing. In the UK in 1981, for instance, over 90 per cent of part-time jobs were held by women; and in other western economies the percentage was nowhere less than 60. A great deal of part-time employment is concentrated in the service sector and this is in some measure a perfectly logical response to the nature of service activity, where hours of work may need to be staggered and where there are sometimes marked fluctuations in service demand over the course of a day.

Part-time employment typically affords much less security than full-time employment and, in this light, women employees may be seen as a disadvantaged group alongside men. There is a corresponding inequality in wage rates, despite long-standing agitation by labour organizations (see Figure 7.10). In UK manufacturing in 1982, for instance, female wages were only 68.8 per cent of male wages. It was Scandinavia, once more, which had made most progress in achieving female equivalence. South Korea exhibited the

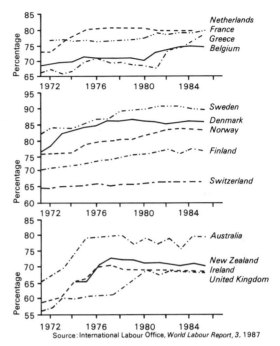

Source: International Labour Office, *World Labour Report*, 3, 1987

Figure 7.10 Female earnings as a percentage of male earnings: industrialized market economies, 1971–85; wage earners in manufacturing

poorest record in 1982: 45.1 per cent. It is essential to stress, of course, that a proportion of such wage differentials may be justified on the grounds of different kinds of work to which higher values may be attached. But beyond this, there can be no doubt that discrimination remains.

Migrant labour

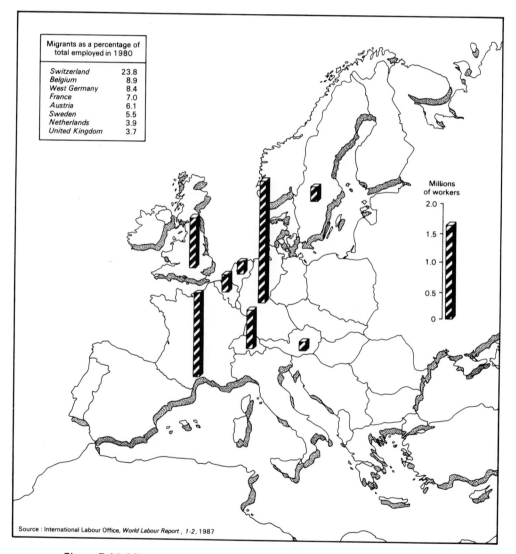

Figure 7.11 Migrant workers in selected western European countries, 1980

The issue of migrant labour has become an emotive one in the later twentieth century. In the past, the presence of foreign labour has been viewed with relative equanimity in the host societies or nations. Many migrant workers brought with them very specific skills – in mining, metallurgy, and textiles, for example. In Europe during the industrial revolution and after, the vitality of some production systems hinged upon such labour influxes. Some have argued that such labour transfers were integral to the industrial transformations in Europe of the later eighteenth and nineteenth centuries.

However, from the Second World War, migrant labour has operated under some very different guises. During the war, the Germans conscripted labour from countries they occupied in order to support the momentum of the German war machine. In South Africa, migrant labour has become a vital prop of industrial production and can be seen to help in sustaining the social system of apartheid. The mining and industrial bases which form the backbone of the contemporary South African economy rely heavily upon the labour of blacks drawn from neighbouring African states. In 1980 there were some 287,000 black foreign workers registered; in mining, they constituted around 40 per cent of the total workforce.

In the industrial west in the post-war era, governments have legislated from time to time to create conditions where an influx of migrant labour and their families is facilitated or actively encouraged. In some instances, this has been an important plank of domestic economic policy: West Germany and Switzerland provide notable cases in point. By 1980, the eight countries of western Europe shown in Figure 7.11 recorded a total of 6.28 million migrant workers. Roughly a third of these were found in West Germany, with Turks representing the largest single ethnic group (almost 29 per cent of the West German total). Out of West Germany's total employment roll

in 1980, migrant labour accounted for some 8.4 per cent. The USA has the largest number of active migrant workers of any single country in the world. Around 1980 the total was some 5 to 6 million. Mexico represents one of the most important source areas; and this encompasses illegal as well as legal immigrants.

Since the 1970s, as unemployment has grown in the industrial west, the issue of migrant labour has become a highly sensitive one. Turkish *Gastarbeiter* in West Germany, for instance, are increasingly viewed as occupying employment which unemployed native Germans might fill. The large-scale growth of foreign workforces of this kind has also given rise to social problems, particularly over their desire to maintain a measure of cultural integrity.

Among middle-income economies and high-income oil exporters, migrant labour has also become an important facet of economic production. In the Arab region of the Middle East (including Libya but excluding Egypt), there were some 2.8 million migrant workers in 1980, just over a million of these in Saudi Arabia. In South America in 1974, there were also some 2.8 million migrant workers, roughly half of them found in Argentina.

The International Labour Office has estimated that in 1980 there were some 20 to 22 million active migrant labourers in the world as a whole. And the definition of a migrant labourer in this case is someone who does not possess citizenship of the country of their employment. When set against the size of the world's labour force, a figure of this kind appears very small. But, as indicated earlier, migrants occupy a decisive economic role in certain host states. In some developing countries, moreover, remittances from emigrant nationals represent a substantial part of national income; this is especially true among some of the smaller states of southern Africa, Lesotho and Botswana among them.

Productivity

One of the hallmarks of capitalist development is the constant search for ways of producing increased returns from a fixed size of capital commitment. The desire for productivity improvement has been a particular pre-occupation of governments of the industrial west in recent decades; similarly, economic researchers and economic commentators have pursued a constant search to identify the key mechanisms of productivity growth. The task was given special impetus during the unfavourable economic climate of the 1970s, when productivity growth in the capitalist west slumped: from an annual average compound rate of 4.5 per cent between 1950 and 1973, to a corresponding rate for 1973 to 1979 of only 2.7 per cent.

The place of human labour in productivity change is one that has been much disputed.

For Marxist commentators, it has to be a primary focus. Labour holds the key to value and it is through manipulations and trans-formations of the labour process that pro-ductivity improvement is attained – whether via the substitution of more efficient machin-ery of manufacture, the streamlining of work practice, more intensive use of shift-working, extending individuals' hours of work, or what-ever. Alternative views do not attach the same importance to labour or the labour process. Here, productivity change is seen to result from a complex of factors, including the state of buoyancy of market demand, levels of accumulated capital stock, the scope for open trading, and so forth. Some of these factors are substitutable, one for the other, and the possible combination of factors is wide, including their relative importance.

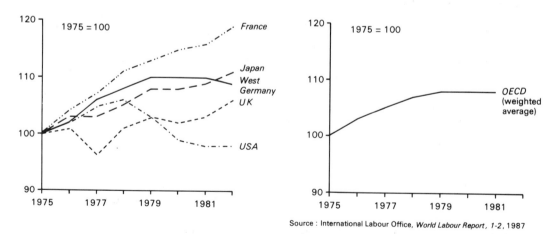

Source : International Labour Office, *World Labour Report, 1-2*, 1987

Figure 7.12 Real wages in manufacturing in leading industrial market economies, 1975–82

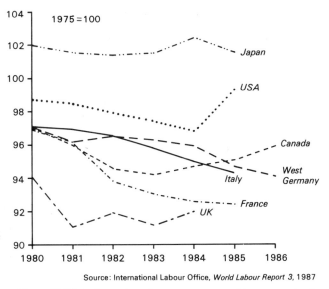

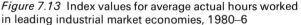

Source: International Labour Office, *World Labour Report 3*, 1987

Figure 7.13 Index values for average actual hours worked in leading industrial market economies, 1980–6

The recent fall in the rate of productivity growth in the capitalist west has been accompanied by a significant fall in real wage improvement. From around 1950 to 1973, wage-earners enjoyed almost continuous enhancement in purchasing power, but after 1973 the pattern tended towards stagnation, even decline in some cases. The picture for the leading industrial market economies from 1975 to 1982 is indicated in Figure 7.12. In both cases, a wage plateau is evident from the late 1970s. The pattern *after* 1982 has shown limited change from this position. West Germany, France, and the UK have exhibited some wage improvement, but in Canada and the USA stagnation has continued.

This adverse trend in real wages was beginning, by the late 1970s, to be mirrored in a change in the number of hours worked. From about 1950 to the mid-1970s, the tendency was for the number of working hours to fall; from 1960, in fact, the pattern had become highly generalized. But between 1978 and 1979, seven industrial market economies registered an *increase* in hours worked; and

the picture for all industrial market economies was of a clear slackening in the downward trend by this date. During the 1980s, these trends have been maintained. Japan, in 1985, registered an index value of 101.6 against a base of 100 in 1975. Australia recorded a corresponding value of 97.5, Sweden of 99.2, and the USA of 99.3. If part-time work is excluded, moreover, the stability of working hours sharpens.

As previously stated, productivity is partly a function of technical capacities, and some of the improvement in labour productivity in the post-war decades can be explained by technical applications. In Europe, in particular, there was a progressive closing of the gap in the adoption of 'best-practice' technology alongside the lead provided in the USA. In 1979, taking US productivity (GDP per man-hour) as a base of 100, fifteen industrial market economies registered an average productivity level of 75; in 1950 the same economies had registered an equivalent value of only 46. In the early 1980s, this upward trend was continued; and it can be related to the secular

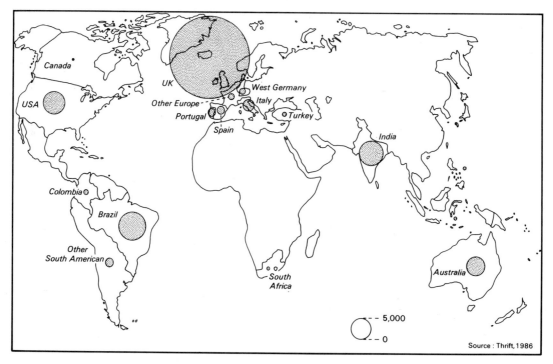

Figure 7.14 World-wide employment in Coats Patons, 1979

growth of unemployment throughout much of the industrialized west, given the context of depressed demand.

Technological substitutions, of course, absorb capital and are not the most attractive propositions in periods of economic instability. An alternative path has thus been to seek to make use of international variations in wage levels. Figures 7.14 and 7.15 take the example of Coats Patons, a multinational textile producer. In 1981, assigning its UK labour costs an index value of 100, the company could demonstrate a range from 134 in Canada to just 6 in Indonesia. Faced with productivity stagnation in the 1970s, the company diversified its locational bases, among other things to take advantage of low labour costs in developing countries. It has now become common to refer to shifts of this kind as expressive of a new international division of labour.

Although wage levels in the developing world are often dramatically lower than in the capitalist west, it has to be pointed out that real wage levels in a number of developing countries have undergone very significant improvement in association with this internationalization of manufacturing production. In Asia, real wages (in regular urban employment) rose at an average annual rate of 1.2 per cent over the years 1971–84; this included rates of 7.8 per cent for South Korea and 4.0 per cent for Singapore. However, in Latin America real wages (in regular urban employment) *fell* by an average of 1.1 per cent per annum between 1971 and 1984. In Africa, moreover, they fell by 3.6 per cent. It is clear that price-inflation accounts for much of this adverse change.

It should be apparent in much of what has been said so far that the search for the controls over labour productivity can rarely proceed much beyond the identification of consistencies of causes and of effects. So complex are the interrelationships of capitalist economic systems that the tracing of paths of even multiple causality is persistently thwarted. It might be logical to assume from this that the task is somewhat less difficult in centrally planned economies, particularly in the industrial socialist states. This is true to an extent, but cause and effect often remain far from distinct, not least because of the causal imperatives of the machinery of central planning. Particular obligations to the state may conflict with, say, the productivity potential of certain technological substitutions. Problems of this kind have been reflected in the 'economic reforms' that have been instituted in the CPEs since the late 1970s. By that date there had been a decisive fall in labour productivity – from 5.5 per cent per annum in 1961–75 to 3.3 per cent over 1976–80. And the pattern intensified from 1981 to 1984 with a recorded value of 2.8 per cent. The benefits of important structural economic changes during the 1950s and 1960s had largely run

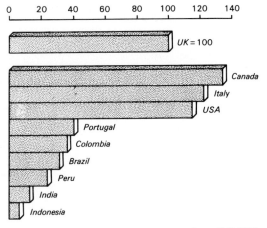

Source : Thrift, 1986

Figure 7.15 Comparative labour costs for Coats Patons world-wide operations in April 1981

their course by this time. A primary target of the reform measures has been an intensification of resource use, involving the establishment of mechanisms capable of overriding the so-called 'dead hand' of state bureaucracy.

Lower Manhattan, New York, USA

8
Multinationals

The nature and scale of foreign direct investment

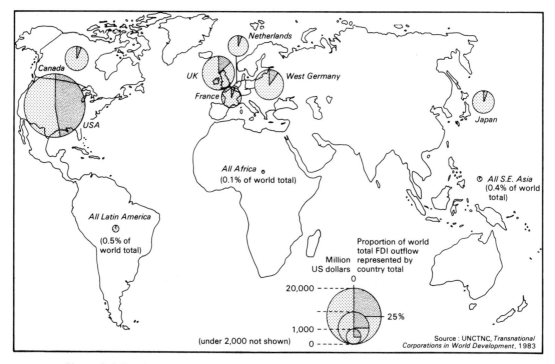

Figure 8.1 Foreign direct investment, 1978–80: outflow of funds (annual average).
The seven countries depicted here accounted for some 94 per cent of the world total FDI outflow
over the period 1978–80. The industrial market economies in aggregate accounted for 99.6 per cent.

The multinational company today occupies a frontal position in capitalist world development. Reference has already been made to the preoccupation in the capitalist realm with rates of economic growth. In the post-war era, multinationals have emerged as growth leaders, sustaining rates of expansion which have often exceeded the collective rates of national economic growth in the core of capitalist nations. Foreign direct investment (FDI) has yielded higher rates of profit than standard home investment. Thus have capitalist relations of production progressively overridden the territoriality of nation-states. During the depression years of the later 1970s and early 1980s, moreover, this process has been aided and abetted (albeit unwittingly) by the actions of such states as they have sought to restrict or slow down the penetration of overseas manufactured goods to protect domestic production capacity, at the same time making available locational incentives for overseas investors in an effort to maximize output growth.

It is conventional to consider the multinational as part of the increasing global organization of production; indeed one of the critical distinguishing features of multinational investment decisions is that they are made from resource appraisals which transgress the largely arbitrary divisions of the world into nation-states of varying geographical scale and economic achievement. For some commentators, the largest multinationals may be likened to nation-states in themselves – by virtue of their having economic assets which vie in size with those of some nation-states proper. Use of the adjective 'global', however, involves considerable licence. In the late 1970s, for instance, roughly three-quarters of total world FDI was found in the developed market economies; moveover, this formed a percentage that was increasing rather than decreasing. Indeed, the sources as well as the destinations of most multinational investment are encompassed within the developed market economies. Japan provides the only significant exception to this pattern, with the greater part of its FDI concentrated in developing market economies. In the socialist realm, foreign direct investment operates under a much more explicitly political umbrella, but its economic impact should not necessarily be viewed any differently from the FDI deriving from the world's market economies. The difficulty, naturally, is that data are much more problematical; although, as many researchers have themselves discovered, the field of MNC investment, generally, is not one that is well-documented.

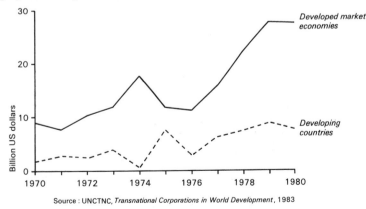

Source : UNCTNC, *Transnational Corporations in World Development*, 1983

Figure 8.2 Inflows of foreign direct investment, 1970–80

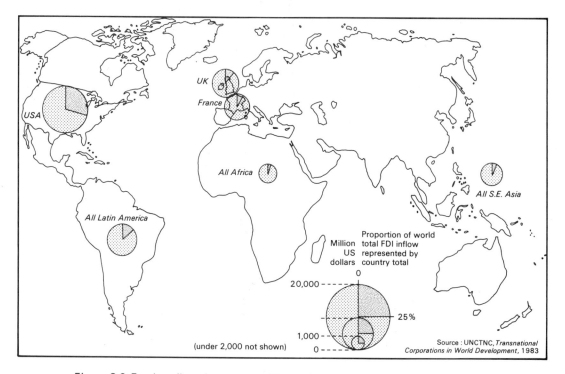

Figure 8.3 Foreign direct investment, 1978–80: inflow of funds (annual average).
This map does not show an exact symmetry with Figure 8.1, but the dominance of the industrial market economies remains. Some 74 per cent of FDI inflow over 1978–80 was destined for these countries.

Multinational enterprise in the world has a fairly long history. Trading organizations such as the East India Company offer important examples of ventures which overrode the singular economic interests of the nation-state, even if, in the East India Company's case, theirs was a trading monopoly which was enshrined in state law. By around 1900, multinational enterprise had extended from trade into manufacturing, perhaps best illustrated by the entry of American firms like Singer into Britain. By virtue of its imperial possessions, Britain maintained the largest share of world FDI up to 1914, but this must necessarily be seen in the context of imperial ties rather than as an illustration of a secular trend in capital organization. The latter was more clearly represented in the emergence of powerful manufacturing combines in Germany and America up to 1914. Thereafter, two world wars and the Great Depression stymied the progress of multinational enterprise. But this was more than compensated from the 1960s as economic output accelerated, as world political conditions became more settled, and as the framework of international business activity became steadily more liberalized. Furthermore, the onset of depressed economic conditions following the oil-price shocks has fed rather than dampened the fires of multinational enterprise, as firms have sought to maintain profits by extending and reconstituting the geographical spreads of their operations.

By the late 1970s, foreign direct investment in the world economy was running at around 42 billion US dollars per annum. By 1978 the world stock of FDI was a little over 400 billion US dollars – roughly equivalent to the UK's gross domestic product in that year. As illustrated already, the USA dominated this investment pattern, representing some 47 per cent of the total in the years 1978–80 (annual average). However, US dominance has in fact declined. In 1970, for instance, it accounted for over half the world total of FDI. Two countries, in particular, have advanced to alter this position: West Germany and Japan. Between 1970 and 1980, Japanese FDI grew sevenfold and West Germany's more than fourfold. By contrast, US FDI little more than doubled.

Something of these trends is apparent in Figure 8.5, which records *net* FDI for all developed market economies between 1970 and 1980 and separate totals for the USA, West Germany, and Japan. Despite the

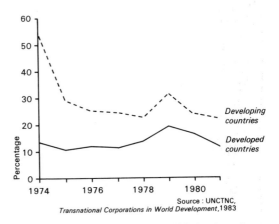

Source : UNCTNC,
*Transnational Corporations in World Development,*1983

Figure 8.4 Rate of return on US foreign direct investment, 1974–81.

The attraction of investing abroad is readily apparent in this graph, although the rate of return on investment in the developing world fell over much of the 1970s.

growing significance of the last-named states, the dominance of the USA is starkly apparent, even if the obvious trend is for the US to

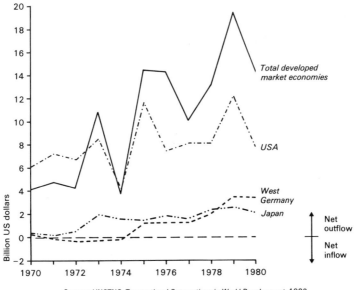

Source : UNCTNC, *Transnational Corporations in World Development,* 1983

Figure 8.5 Net flows of foreign direct investment, 1970–80, for developed market economies

be superseded by the aggregate of developed market economies rather than the reverse. The distinction between net and gross flows of FDI is an important one. Not only does it assist in underlining the symmetric character of much FDI – among the developed market economies, many exporters of capital are at the same time recipients – but it also exposes more acutely the states which hold the greater measure of autonomy in the disposition and control of FDI on a world scale.

The scale of FDI is, of course, but one measure of the way in which capitalist relations of production have spread across national boundaries. Given the importance of multinationals in this process, it is clearly appropriate to look at the rate of formation of overseas manufacturing subsidiaries. It is these that constitute the spearhead of 'global' production and which have done so much to alter the framework within which locational

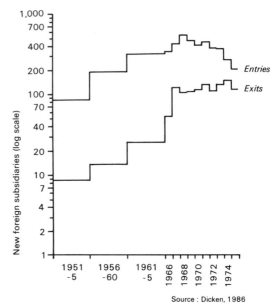

Source : Dicken, 1986

Figure 8.6 Foreign manufacturing subsidiaries of US multinationals, 1951–75

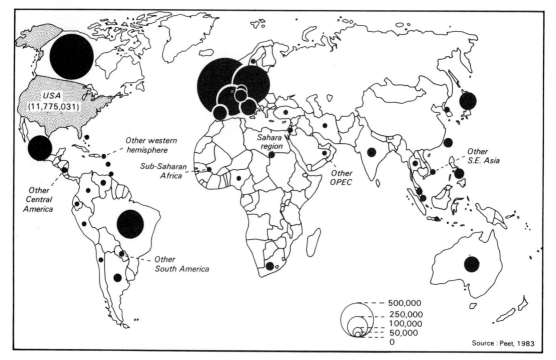

Figure 8.7 Employment in manufacturing by US corporations

behaviour is now studied. Figure 8.6 indicates entries and exits (births and deaths) for overseas manufacturing subsidiaries of US multinationals from 1951 to 1975. In the early 1950s, formation rates were just under 100 per annum. Shortly prior to the oil-price shock of 1973–4, this figure had risen to settle between 400 and 500 per annum, a level clearly consistent with the USA as the source of over half world FDI at the time. After the oil-price shock, though, formation rates slipped back, while exit rates, which had been accelerating, remained roughly stable. The obvious implication is that this change sprang from the contemporary world recession, but such an explanation should not be emphasized too strongly. It may also have arisen from an increase in the unit size of overseas subsidiaries, the more so given the contemporary growth in US FDI over the course of the 1970s.

Whatever the scale of investment or the numerical strength of subsidiaries, the power and influence of multinationals also derives from the proportionate significance that they are able to command within host countries in terms of employment, production, and, more widely, competitive momentum. According to the International Labour Office, some 44 million people were employed directly by multinationals in 1980. Although this amounts to only 2.5 per cent of the world's total labour force, the concentration of multinational investment in the industrial market economies means that the real significance of the figure was considerably greater, possibly as high as 10 per cent. Predictably, the USA dominates this pattern, with an international labour force in manufacturing alone of some 4.3 million in 1980, that is about one-fifth the size of the domestic force. The geographical distribution of these employees is illustrated in Figure 8.7. The importance of industrial market economies as host nations is immediately apparent here; Brazil and Mexico offer the only exceptions of any note.

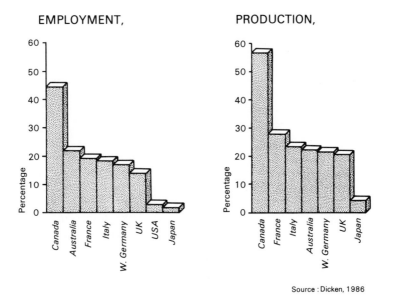

Source : Dicken, 1986

Figure 8.8 Foreign share of national manufacturing employment and production, 1970s

The degree to which multinational investment at large is supportive of domestic *employment* bases in the industrial market economies is depicted in Figure 8.8, which shows the pattern over the 1970s. For Canada, 44.3 per cent of manufacturing employment derived from FDI; in Australia, the corresponding total was 22 per cent. Japan reveals the most limited involvement: a mere 1.8 per cent. In the developing economies, Brazil registered a corresponding value of 30 per cent and Mexico 21 per cent, although such figures must necessarily be viewed in the context of a youthful manufacturing sector, one which in some instances has been spearheaded through multinational involvement. In the realm of manufacturing *production,* the contribution of multinationals emerges even more strongly than in employment, as Figure 8.8 shows. For Canada, 56.6 per cent of manufacturing production in the 1970s was attributable to foreign investors. In France the figure was 27.8 per cent. These values, as well as those for employment, tend to relate to limited sectors of the manufacturing spectrum where multinational enterprise has found the scope for investment most profitable. This facet has tended to enhance the bargaining position of multinationals in the face of ambivalent government attitudes; and in cases it has

sharpened the impact of labour militancy. Sectoral concentration also involves geographical concentration and thus lends a higher public profile to potential investment gain or loss. Domination of any single production sector in a country frequently brings with it a facility to 'pace' the market and to secure some of the benefit of monopoly conditions. Moreover, this is a dimension which may be readily exploited *internationally* – for instance, by deliberately slowing the rate of technology transfer from parent company to overseas subsidiary in order to maximize returns from standing capital investments.

Finally, one other measure of the significance of FDI is the share that it forms of gross fixed capital formation in single nation-states. The position in 1982–3 in the developed world is illustrated in Figure 8.10. For the industrial market economies as a whole, the figure was 2.9 per cent. However, this disguised wide variations. For Japan, the figure was a minimal 0.1 per cent, whereas for Belgium and Australia it was 8.4 and 6.9 per cent respectively. In broad terms there appears to be an inverse relationship between the level of FDI as a percentage of gross fixed capital formation and the level of GNP per capita. Thus the USA, France, and West Germany record low levels, whereas Spain, Ireland, and Greece record high levels. However, neither Australia nor Belgium really fits this pattern.

No discussion of foreign direct investment or of the role of multinationals would be complete without commenting on the difficulties involved in acquiring accurate data. This has become notably true with the growth of *conglomerate* multinationals, where there is no common manufacturing or 'product' base. Firms are bought up, financial stakes acquired, and affiliate relations established on the strength of general investment considerations. Sometimes these interests are not easily or wholly identifiable. Moreover, the task is made doubly difficult by the pace of

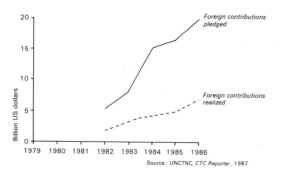

Figure 8.9 Cumulative foreign direct investment in China, 1979–86.

China: the latest frontier in World FDI, absorbing roughly a billion US dollars per annum in the first half of the 1980s.

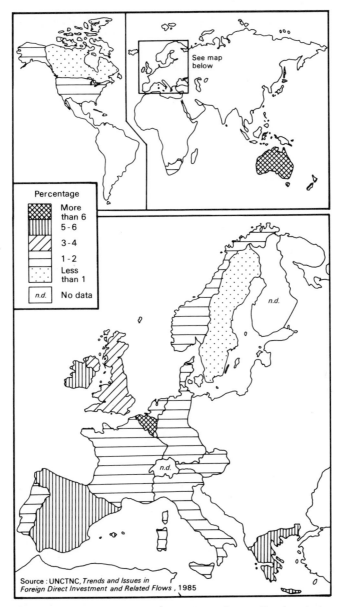

Figure 8.10 Inflows of FDI as a share of gross fixed capital formation: industrial market economies, 1982–3

change. The international capitalist world may be characterized by explosive energy but it is also a world in permanent flux. Thus the charts and maps on these pages are but snapshots, and in that respect but poor communicators of international capitalist evolution.

155

The corporate giants

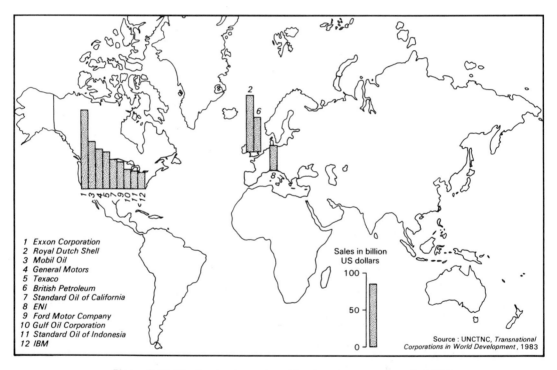

Figure 8.11 The twelve largest multinational corporations in 1980

For the average layman, the term multinational corporation calls to mind such firms as General Motors, Texaco, and International Business Machines (IBM). If one examines the commodity sectors occupied by the world's largest MNCs, oil proves by far the most significant, a position which can be directly associated with the enormous growth in international oil exchange as a consequence of the strong mismatch between the geography of oil production and of consumption. If one measures the strength of MNCs by their sales values, eight out of the twelve largest industrial MNCs in 1980 were based in oil. And, predictably, the percentage of sales outside the host state was high – for instance, 77.6 per cent for BP, 69.1 per cent for Mobil, and 68.6 per cent for Texaco. Of these twelve giant corporations, no less than nine were US-based, reflecting the general domination of the USA in world FDI described earlier. As repositories of wealth, the world's largest MNCs do indeed vie with nation-states. For example, in 1980 the Exxon Corporation, BP, and Royal Dutch Shell together had assets roughly equivalent to the Swiss gross domestic product in that year. BP's assets alone exceeded the GDPs of both New Zealand and Ireland. In terms of the labour that they command, however, the oil companies fall second place to the vehicle producers. In 1980, General Motors had a world-wide workforce of three-quarters of a million, 30 per cent of them outside of the USA. The Exxon Corporation could boast only 177,000, even if over half were overseas.

It is logical to presume that the financial strength of these giant multinationals has flowed in substantial part from a continuing capacity to invade and extend foreign markets. And if one examines foreign sales (i.e. sales outside the host state) as a share of total sales, this appears to be the case. In 1971, for all industrial sectors, the percentage was 30. It rose to 35 per cent in 1976 and 40 per cent in 1980. The pattern for individual industrial sectors by 1980 is indicated in Figure 8.12. Petroleum registered the highest value (49 per cent); it also recorded the greatest rate of increase – 28 percentage points from 1971.

One of the obvious results of the emergence of international industrial organization and production is that more and more international trading is likely to take place within

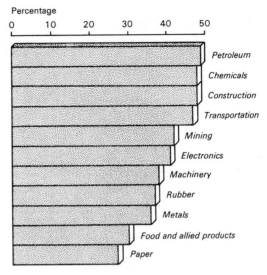

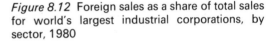

Source : UNCTNC, *Transnational Corporations in World Development*, 1983

Figure 8.12 Foreign sales as a share of total sales for world's largest industrial corporations, by sector, 1980

the realm of single firms. In the USA in 1977, for instance, 45.5 per cent of the exports of large industrial corporations could be classified as intra-firm. For the industrial market economies as a whole in 1977, the average was 32.8 per cent. In some cases, this is a simple question of the transfer of semi-finished goods or manufactured parts in the conventional fashion of industrial organization where there is a spatial separation of production processes. But one of the critical facilities of multinational organization is the ability to treat saleable stocks on a world-wide basis. Thus finished goods, in whatever national locations they are stored, become accessible to meet demand in any of a multinational's foreign locations. What is more, such goods can be moved largely without regard to prevailing market prices. In a sense, the multinational has the capacity to create its own internal market. And it is in this light that some have argued for viewing MNCs rather as economic equivalents of nation-states.

Foreign direct investment in the developing world

The relocation of multinational industrial production to areas of the developing world is a facet much commented upon. This is especially true when it can be argued to be part of the 'new international division of labour' whereby mass-production industries and manufacturing sectors which remain relatively labour-intensive (like clothing) capitalize on the diminutive power of labour in Third World countries as regards wages, conditions, and combination. It remains to stress, however, that the developing world receives a relatively minor share of total world FDI. Over the years 1978–80, its share was only 30.7 per cent of that of the industrial market economies. Admittedly, this investment was concentrated in a limited number of countries in specific parts of the world. Over 1978–80, for instance, Latin America took some 61 per cent of FDI in the developing world, SE Asia and Oceania a further 30 per cent. But if one examines the scale of FDI in these developing regions relative to the scale of their domestic investment, the picture is one of relatively limited significance, as Figure 8.13 demonstrates. When one begins to analyse the specific targets of FDI in Latin America, of course, the pattern that emerges is somewhat different. In Brazilian automobile production, for instance, foreign domination is total. In chemicals in 1977, 54 per cent of sales were accounted for by foreign firms; in industrial

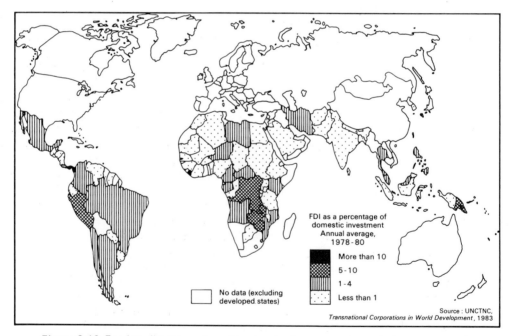

Figure 8.13 Foreign direct investment in developing countries relative to domestic investment, 1978–80

machinery the parallel figure was 59 per cent. Across all Brazilian manufacturing sectors, the average for 1977 was 44 per cent. And the equivalent statistics on fixed assets, on equity, and on employment paint a very similar picture.

It is clear that assessments of the role of multinational enterprise in the developing world are not made easily. On the one hand, there is an inherent tendency to treat terms like 'global organization of production' and 'new international division of labour' as indicators of a state that has been realized rather than the predicted outcomes of prevailing trends. On the other hand, the formidable influence that some corporations exert in defined spheres is inescapable. And one of the most telling illustrations of this lies not in their scale of investment or in the degree of their industrial domination, but in the shares of developing countries' exports that they control. The size of the shares held by the fifteen largest multinationals in leading export sectors in 1980 are depicted in Figure 8.14. Forest products were by far the most significant of developing countries' exports, valued at 54.4 billion US dollars in 1980. The percentage marketed by the fifteen largest multinationals, as the chart reveals, was 90. Similar levels of control applied in coffee and corn exports. Given the extent to which agriculture dominates the export profiles of many developing countries (in Africa in the mid-1980s the level was still nearly 50 per cent), this clearly represents an undesirable monopoly, although how *far* such countries would themselves be able to secure more advantageous terms of trade is uncertain.

Another problematical facet of FDI in the developing world is the tendency to concentrate on the 'better-off' or on the less poor. Over 1978–80, some 50 per cent of FDI flows from industrial market economies went to countries with more than 1,000 US dollars per capita GNP. This immediately excludes all low-income economies, following the World

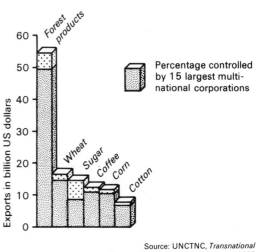

Source: UNCTNC, *Transnational Corporations in World Development,* 1983

Figure 8.14 Shares of developing countries' exports controlled by multinational corporations, 1980

Bank classification; it also excludes many middle-income economies.

One of the most commonly cited spheres of MNC domination in the developing world is non-ferrous metal mining and refining. And when one examines, for example, world capacities in aluminium, alumina, and bauxite production, the outcome is in little doubt. In 1982, the six largest MNCs controlled 44.5 per cent of world aluminium capacity, 50.4 per cent of world alumina capacity, and 46.3 per cent of world bauxite capacity. By contrast, the governments of developing countries, where most mine production is located, recorded corresponding values of 5 per cent, 6.3 per cent, and 19.3 per cent respectively. However, the picture is not the same in all non-ferrous metals. In copper, for instance, the post-war decades have seen a progressive slide in the control wielded by the bigger multinationals. In 1948, the top seven companies accounted for 70 per cent of world production, but in 1981 this figure had slipped to only 23 per cent. In tin, much the same pattern has prevailed.

United Kingdom foreign direct investment

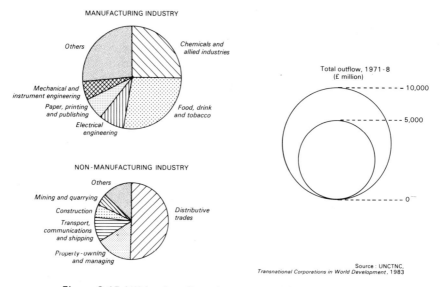

Figure 8.15 UK foreign direct investment, 1971–8 (by sector)

The United Kingdom has a long tradition of overseas investment. With the break-up of its empire and the economic rise of countries like West Germany and Japan it no longer dominates world FDI as it once did, but the absolute scale of UK FDI has continued to grow in relatively uninterrupted fashion. Over the years 1971–8, the total flow of investment overseas was £12.5 billion, roughly 82 per cent of this destined for other industrial market economies, notably the USA and countries of the EEC. By the 1980s, the political gibe of the Labour Party opposition that, in manufacturing, Britain was on the way to becoming a warehouse economy had more than just a ring of truth about it. This derived not just from a high level of imports of basic manufactured goods and a reciprocal depletion of domestic production capacity. It came also from a decline in manufacturing for export and its replacement by manufacturing investment overseas, working largely within an unchanged market arena.

Figure 8.15 demonstrates the sectoral split of UK FDI over the years 1971–8. The division between manufacturing and non-manufacturing was roughly 2:1. Within the manufacturing sector, chemicals and allied industries, and food, drink, and tobacco accounted for 55 per cent of all investment, effectively contradicting the oft-held belief that most FDI is focused on high-technology sectors. In non-manufacturing industry, over half the investment was found in the distributive trades, a facet clearly consistent with high levels of investment in the food, drink, and tobacco industries, for example.

The geographical distribution of UK FDI is illustrated in Figure 8.16. Apart from the concentration in the USA and western

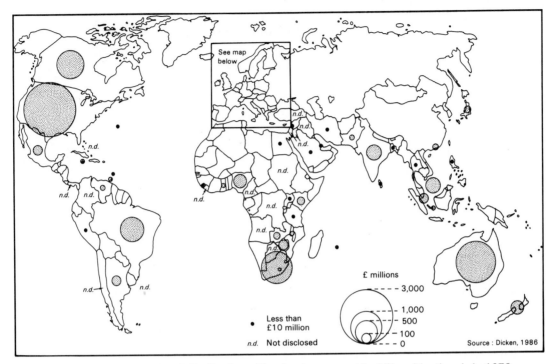

Figure 8.16 Geographical distribution of foreign investment by UK multinationals in 1978

Europe, the pattern is notable for its reflections of empire. With the exception of Brazil, all remaining major investment foci lie in countries of the Commonwealth (including South Africa, which formally withdrew in 1960). Of the major contributors to world FDI, the UK demonstrates perhaps the widest geographical spread, although the trend has been for this to lessen.

If one focuses just on UK FDI in the *developing* world, the sectoral concentration that emerges is not altogether different from that in the developed. In manufacturing over the years 1971–8, some 36 per cent of overseas investment was in food, drink, and tobacco; there was a further 23 per cent in chemicals and allied products. In non-manufacturing industry, the distributive trades took 70 per cent of FDI. In other words, the world-wide sectoral pattern was even more clearly marked in the developing world.

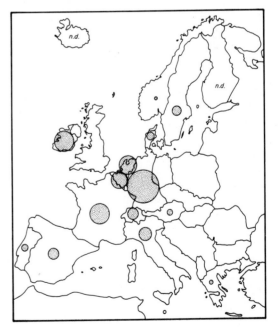

Japanese foreign direct investment

The economic rise of Japan and the country's increasing force in the world economic system have been recurrent features throughout this book. In foreign direct investment, although comparatively late of entry, Japan has demonstrated a vigour which has more than matched its record performances in most other economic spheres. Before the mid-1960s, the Japanese economy had little apparent need to invest abroad; and, besides, there were strict government controls over overseas capital investment. After the 1960s, however, this pattern began to alter radically. Japanese FDI, which had averaged only 73.5 million US dollars over the years 1951–66, jumped to an annual average of 1.9 billion dollars between 1967 and 1977. By 1978–80, the parallel figure was 4.76 billion. If one examines the *net* FDI position, moreover, the picture is not much changed (see Figure 8.17), since Japan is far more a source than a destination of FDI. In 1983, for instance, while the USA recorded a net inflow of 6.88 billion dollars, Japan recorded a net outflow of 3.1 billion, a figure exceeded only by Canada. On a cumulative basis, Japanese FDI in 1978 represented some 7 per cent of the world total.

The sectoral distribution of Japanese FDI over the time-span 1951–80 shows important differences alongside the pattern in some leading western nations. For example, extrac-

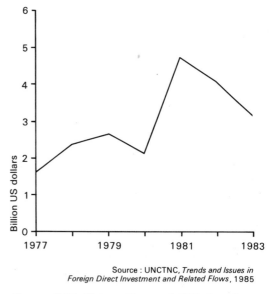

Source : UNCTNC, *Trends and Issues in Foreign Direct Investment and Related Flows*, 1985

Figure 8.17 Net outflow of FDI for Japan, 1977–83

tive industry, in which mining is overwhelmingly dominant, accounted for nearly 22 per cent, an obvious reflection of the dearth of industrial raw materials in Japan and the necessity to import heavily. Similarly, the service sector is unusually prominent (43.6 per cent), in very evident contrast to the sectoral pattern in the UK. Within manufacturing, though, there is a continuing prominence for

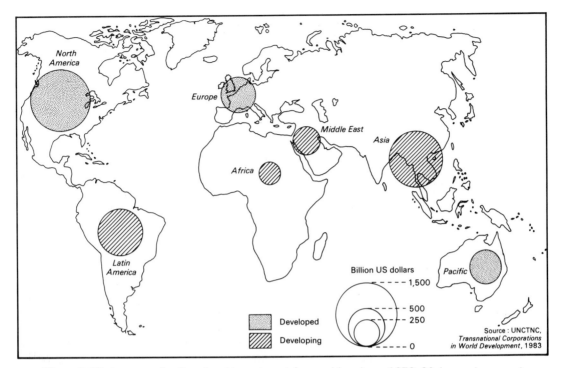

Figure 8.18 Japanese foreign direct investment, by world regions, 1978–80 (annual average)

the more basic producing sectors like textiles, metals, and electrical machinery: together these accounted for 46 per cent of the manu- facturing total; chemicals represented a further 21 per cent.

Another distinguishing characteristic of Japanese FDI is its prominence in the devel- oping world. Approximately half of Japanese overseas investment over the years 1978–80 was directed towards developing countries. Asia in turn absorbed roughly half of this, Latin America approximately one-third. Over the decade 1967–77, much the same division operated. Japan's investment in the devel- oping world has been highest in textiles and chemicals, lowest in commerce, finance, and insurance. In extractive industry and in manufacturing, generally, it was as high as 66 per cent. In services, by contrast, the figure was only 37 per cent.

It is tempting to rationalize the geographical pattern of Japanese FDI in simple terms of spatial proximity, at least as far as the focus on Asia and on the developing world is con- cerned. And, in so far as this bears some coincidence with the old Japanese Empire, there is further merit in the interpretation. The prominence of the USA as a destination for investment in the developed world might be seen to reflect the role of American econ- omic and political assistance in post-war Japanese reconstruction. However, such explanations must be subsumed within an analysis which examines first the evolving format of the capitalist relations of production in post-war Japan. By the later 1960s, Japan's economic recovery was achieving a momen- tum that could be sustained only through outward investment. The particular form of that capital export revolved around the characteristics of production at home and this has remained largely the pattern since.

The service sector

The importance of the service sector in Japanese FDI reflects what has been a rising trend in world FDI in the 1970s and 1980s: that is, the growing internationalization of business services. This includes trading, banking, accounting, advertising, insurance, and legal services. Moreover, the growth of FDI in services can be directly related to the expansion of FDI in industry and manufacturing. The emergence of industrial multinationals created a growing demand for an international array of business services. This is not in any sense to say that other factors, such as the rise of international currency markets or the general growth in international trade, have not been important. It is simply to identify industrial MNCs as the prime catalyst. Yet a further ingredient in this development has been the revolution in information technology, which has effectively annihilated the inhibiting influence of geographical space. For example, the stockmarkets of London, Hong Kong, Tokyo, and New York hold geographical significance only in so far as they lie in different world time-zones. The dawn of the electronic age has made possible the growth of the truly international business community, characterized by instantaneous information transfer and split-second decision-making, regardless of geographical locale.

The stock of FDI in the service sector in the USA and in West Germany over the years 1973–83 is illustrated in Figure 8.19. In 1973, services accounted for 18.4 per cent of the total stock of FDI in the USA and 17.5 per cent in West Germany. By 1983, the parallel figures were 25.3 per cent and 24.9 per cent. At the forefront of FDI in services has been the banking sector. By the late-1970s, US transnational banks had some 700 overseas branches, against a figure of around 100 immediately after the Second World War. Predictably, transnational banking assets dwarf those of industrial multinationals. In 1980, BP boasted the largest assets of any industrial MNC: 29.9 billion US dollars. But even in 1975, Citicorp, the giant US international bank, had assets of 87.1 billion dollars; by 1985 these had doubled to 167.2 billion. In 1975, the top ten transnational banks (based on total assets) included only two from Japan. By 1985, the power of Japanese international banking had grown at such a pace that it occupied ranks 2, 3, 4, 5, and 7. In other words, in yet another field of the world capitalist economy, the Japanese have forged a position of world domination in a breathtakingly short time.

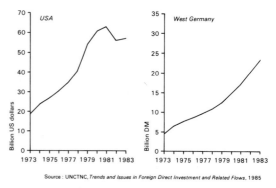

Source: UNCTNC, *Trends and Issues in Foreign Direct Investment and Related Flows*, 1985

Figure 8.19 Stock of FDI in the service sector at year end, 1973–83, USA and West Germany

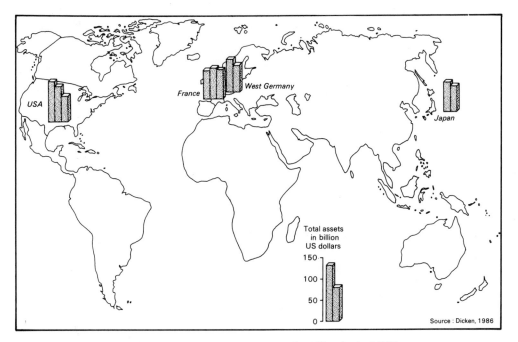

Figure 8.20 The top ten transnational banks in 1975

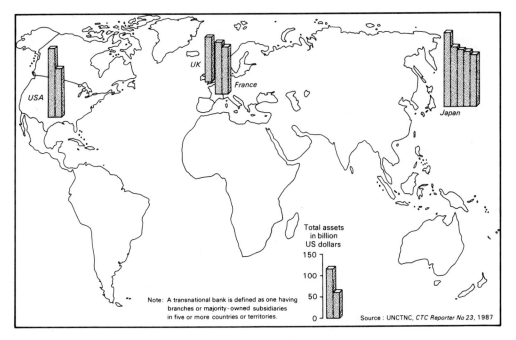

Figure 8.21 The top ten transnational banks in 1985

References

Statistical reports and compendia

Eurostat *Energy Statistical Yearbook*, Luxemburg.

FAO (Food and Agriculture Organization of the United Nations) *Production Yearbook*, Rome

FAO (1977) *Fourth World Food Survey*, Rome

FAO (1984, 1985) *The State of Food and Agriculture*, Rome

FAO *Trade Yearbook*, Rome

HMSO *Employment Gazette*, London

International Energy Agency (1987) *Energy Prices and Taxes*, Paris

International Labour Office (1987) *World Labour Report*, Geneva

International Labour Office *Yearbook of Labour Statistics*, Geneva

Metal Bulletin Ltd *Handbook*, Worcester Park, England

Metal Bulletin Ltd *Prices and Data*, Worcester Park, England

Society of Motor Manufacturers and Traders *The Motor Industry of Great Britain*, London

The Economist *The World in Figures*, London

UN (United Nations) *Demographic Yearbook*, New York

UN *Statistical Yearbook*, New York

UN *World Economic Survey*, New York

UN *Yearbook of Industrial Statistics*, New York

UN *Yearbook of World Energy Statistics*, New York

UNCTNC (United Nations Centre for Transnational Corporations) (1983) *Transnational Corporations in World Development*, New York

UNCTNC *CTC Reporter*, New York

UNCTNC (1985) *Trends and Issues in Foreign Direct Investment and Related Flows*, New York

World Bank *World Development Reports*, Oxford

World Resources Institute (1986, 1987) *World Resources*, New York

Books and journals

Bloomfield, G. T. (1981) 'The changing spatial organization of multinational corporations in the world automotive industry'. In F. E. I. Hamilton and G. J. R. Linge (eds) *Spatial Analysis, Industry and the Industrial Environment: 2: International Industrial Systems*, pp. 357–94, Chichester

Dacharry, M. (1981) *Géographie du Transport Aérien*, Paris

Dicken, P. (1986) *Global Shift: Industrial Change in a Turbulent World*, London

Grigg, D. (1985) *The World Food Problem*, Oxford

Hedley, D. (1986) *World Energy: the Facts and the Future,* London

Leung, C. K. (1980) *China: Railway Patterns and National Goals,* Chicago

Maddison, A. (1982) *Phases of Capitalist Development,* Oxford

Malenbaum, W. (1978) *World Demand for Raw Materials in 1985 and 2000,* New York

Odell, P. R. (1986) 'Draining the world of energy'. In R. J. Johnston and P. J. Taylor (eds) *A World in Crisis? Geographical Perspectives,* pp. 68–88, Oxford

Peet, R. (1983) 'Relations of production and the relocation of United States manufacturing industry since 1960', *Economic Geography* 59: 112–43.

Thrift, N. (1986) 'The geography of international economic disorder'. In R. J. Johnston and P. J. Taylor (eds) *A World in Crisis? Geographical Perspectives,* pp. 12–67, Oxford

Woods, R. I. (1986) 'Malthus, Marx and population crises'. In R. J. Johnston and P. J. Taylor (eds) *A World in Crisis? Geographical Perspectives,* pp. 127–49, Oxford

Zachariah, K. C. and S. Patel (1984) 'Determinants of fertility decline in India: an analysis', *World Bank Staff Working Paper* No. 699.

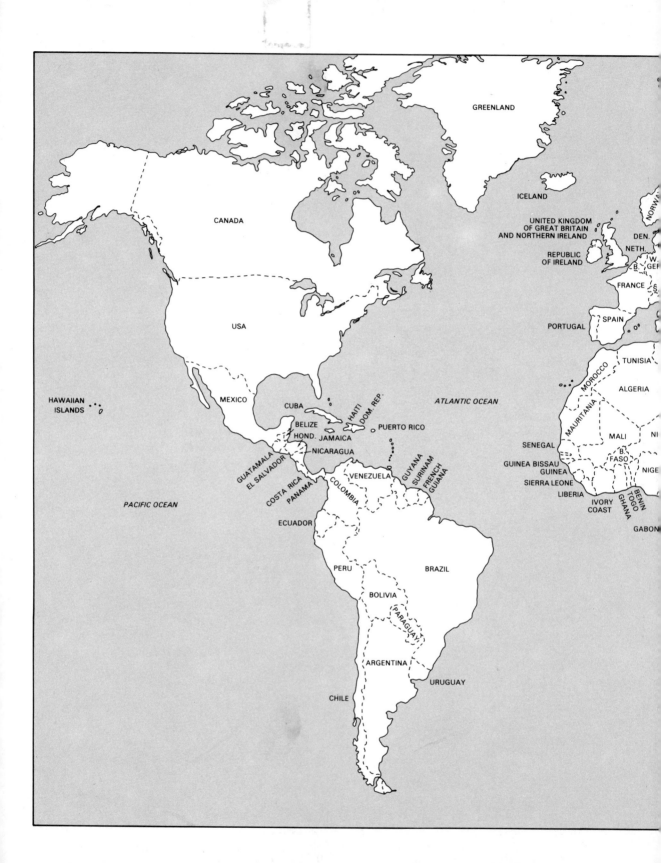